Transforming the
Primary School

Transforming the Primary School

JOHN BLACKIE

SCHOCKEN BOOKS • NEW YORK

First SCHOCKEN edition 1974

Copyright © 1974 by John Blackie
Published in Great Britain under the title *Changing the Primary School*
Manufactured in the United States of America

Library of Congress Cataloging in Publication Data

Blackie, John Haldane, 1904-
  Transforming the primary school.

  Includes bibliographical references.
  1. Education, Elementary—Great Britain.
I. Title.
LA633.B53   372.9'42   73-91336

Contents

Preface

In December, 1970, there met together for a fortnight at Weston-super-Mare, Somerset, England, a number of educationalists from many parts of the world. The object of the meeting, which was held under the auspices of the Centre for Educational Development Overseas (CEDO), the United Nations Educational, Scientific and Cultural Organisation (UNESCO) and the British Council, was to consider and learn more about the English primary school and, in particular, the practice that has become known as the integrated day.

I was invited to attend and take part in the proceedings and then to write a book arising out of them. Nothing more precise was indicated. I was given a completely free hand.

A great many books have been written about the English primary school, including one with the title *The Integrated Day*.[1] There is a whole series of pamphlets on the subject, published by Macmillan under the auspices of the Ford Foundation. I did not want just to add another book to compete in an overcrowded market. Listening to what was said and discussing with the various delegates the problems and practices of their own countries, I came to the conclusion that there was a place for a short introductory book which dealt specifically with the process of change, with the reasons for change, with what might and might not be expected of it, with preparation for it, with the conditions that make it possible. The reader that I have had mainly in mind is someone without direct experience of modern English primary practice, with a mind open to the possibility of change and with a strong determination not to change unless good reasons can be shown for it. Such a reader may be a politician, an administrator, an

7

inspector or a teacher, or a member of the general public with an interest in education.

I have described my own experience, stated my own convictions and tried to show on what they are founded. What I have said in no way commits my friends of the Weston-super-Mare conference or its sponsors to agreement. It is not a summary of their views but, in writing it, I have had continuously in mind what they said and what they have told me about their countries and educational systems. I should like to hope that the book will make a small contribution to those systems and through them to the children whom they serve, as well as to primary education in my own country.

I should like to express my gratitude to Robert and Jenny Balchin and to Seona Denholm and Carol Dasgupta, all practising teachers and the two latter former students of mine at Homerton, for having read the book in typescript and for many valuable suggestions; also to my former colleague Gilbert Peaker for help with certain statistical matters. I am grateful, too, to Elizabeth Taylor and to Messrs Methuen and Co. Ltd for permission to quote from *Experiments with a Backward Class*.

Author's note

In writing this book I have used the terminology familiar to English readers. Some of this will be strange to readers of other nationalities and the following short glossary may be useful.

Infant School For children of 5 to 7, sometimes containing a *Nursery Class* for 4-year-olds. May be a separate school or, in rural areas, simply part of a *Junior School* (see below). The Plowden Council suggested the name *First School* but this is only very slowly coming into use.

Junior School For children of 7 to 11+. The Plowden Council recommended that children should spend an additional year in the *First School* and remain in the Junior School until they were 12. The *Junior School* was then to be called the *Middle School*. This change is steadily taking place, but the old term is still widely used.

Integrated This term is quite unconnected with multi-racial schools. It is rather loosely used. Its meaning in this book is described in Chapter 4.

Streaming In the US known as *tracking*. It means the practice, in large schools, of classifying an age-group in two or more parallel classes, selected according to ability.

Selection Examination In 1926 the Hadow Report proposed that, at the age of 11 or thereabouts, children should sit an examination, often popularly called the eleven-plus, in which the most successful (the percentage varied from area to area) were then transferred to *Grammar Schools* with a more or less

9

academic curriculum, while the remainder went to *Senior Elementary Schools*, later rechristened *Secondary Modern Schools*, where the curriculum was more varied, more practical, and intellectually less demanding. This system is now dying, slowly in some areas, more rapidly in others, and is being replaced by a non-selective transfer to *Comprehensive Schools*.

O Levels The *General Certificate of Education* (*GCE*) is the examination in most common use in secondary schools. It is divided into Ordinary Level and Advanced Level stages. Hence, 'I'm taking my O Levels this year.' There is also the *Certificate of Secondary Education* (*CSE*), a rather easier examination organised on a different basis.

HM Inspectors This corps of men and women was first formed in 1839 and for many years the inspectors were the sole agents for the evaluation of teachers' work and for the support and guidance of their efforts. From 1867 to 1898 they conducted annual examinations in the schools. They now fulfil mainly an advisory role and, to the regret of many, spend less time in classrooms than formerly. (See John Blackie: *Inspecting and the Inspectorate*, Routledge and Kegan Paul, London, 1970.)

Progressive The word in most general use, both by friends and enemies, to indicate very broadly the kind of practices described in this book.

Course books Textbooks containing courses or programmes which the teacher and his class may follow, e.g. in the English language.

Chapter 1
What is rejected

The assumption on which this book is written is that primary schools ought to be changed. If this is so, it is essential to be clear about the nature of the situation which needs changing and about why it is believed that a change is necessary. The situation is in no sense uniform. Primary education in different countries is in different stages of development and in the United Kingdom, where development has gone further than anywhere else, there is a wide difference between schools which have moved ahead and those which have lagged behind.

Nevertheless, it is possible, and may be useful, to state in general terms the kind of practices against which those who desire a change are rebelling. At the very outset it must be said that they are not rebelling against hard work, sound learning or systematic knowledge. Critics of the approach upheld in this book have often accused it of endangering or ignoring these, and teachers who have adopted the approach without understanding it have presented them with free ammunition. It must be plainly stated that the approach is recommended because, properly made, it obtains better results in every relevant particular than the one that is being rejected. This claim is expanded and supported in later chapters.

A further preliminary remark is necessary. It is not assumed that whatever changes are made will be made instantaneously by decree or that they can be so made. The move from the old to the new must be made at the speed which the circumstances justify and, more specifically, according to the state of teacher training in the country concerned. A premature attempt to transform a national system, before the teaching force was ready for it, would inevitably end in calamity.

What then is to be rejected? First in importance though not in time, the programme. By this word is meant a syllabus, a methodology, a plan of work, an outline of study drawn up by some central authority, no matter how enlightened, and then imposed upon the teachers. It is not, for present purposes, important how good this programme is. It may be out of date and uninteresting or it may be modern, sophisticated, supported by every kind of apparatus and device and full of interest. It is rejected simply because it is a programme, because it denies the initiative, imagination and inventiveness of the teacher in contact with the child. In most countries this change, the rejection of the programme, would be revolutionary. In the United Kingdom, where the rejection occurred in 1926, the resultant changes in attitudes and practices are still far from complete. If the change is to be made, it must be very carefully planned, its implications thought out and a long transitional period allowed for.

It should be said at once that teachers need help, that some teachers need a lot of help and that some of the help given may resemble a programme. This will be discussed in Chapter 13. In the meantime the vital difference between the programme and the 'help' to keep in mind is that the former is pre-packaged and mandatory and the latter suggestive and non-compulsory.

Secondly, the fixed subdivided time-table or schedule must be rejected. Such a time-table divides the school day into compartments, and lays down, sometimes in great detail, what is to be done in each compartment and precisely how long each compartment is to last. In some countries this type of time-table is centrally determined, so that the Minister of Education is able to look at his watch and say: 'At this moment every child in Grade X is doing division of fractions.' Some ministers could add: 'And, if any inspector finds a teacher doing anything else, that teacher will be in trouble.' But a time-table can be just as rigid if it is drawn up by the head teacher. In the United Kingdom time-tables of this kind were almost universal before the Second World War and, though much less common now, are not extinct.

What is rejected is, first, the belief implied in such time-tables, that it is desirable for anybody to decide what it is best for all children to be doing at any given moment and how long they ought to go on doing it. Secondly, what is rejected is the compartmenting of subject matter, the subdivision of knowledge and study into separate disciplines. This change, which is crucial, has been much misunderstood and it will be well to dispose of some of the misunderstandings before going further.

Some supporters of integration—the word generally used for the results of rejecting compartmentalisation—have asserted that all knowledge is one. This is certainly not so. There are different kinds of knowledge and different ways of acquiring knowledge. The methods used in studying and acquiring knowledge of science are largely quite different from those appropriate to literature. Much intellectual advance has, in fact, taken the form of differentiating between branches of knowledge, of, for example, removing astrology from the bounds of astronomy, herbalism from botany, cosmography from theology. But there is a sense in which study does, indeed must, ignore the boundaries of disciplines if it is to be meaningful. This is particularly true of study by young children of the age with which this book is concerned.

A child looking at an ancient building will certainly ask questions which belong to the disciplines of history, theology, engineering and mathematics—'Who built it? What was it for? What is it made of? How big is it? How did they put the stones up? How are the bricks made?' These questions may all be turned to good account in the process of educating him. Nor will he have anything to unlearn later on, when he begins to concentrate upon one subject himself and to realise that it is impossible for anyone to pursue all subjects or to possess all skills.

Third to be rejected is the assumption that children are not willing learners. No one with any knowledge of very young children could possibly make such an assumption unqualified, yet it is very widely made and is implicit and sometimes explicit in many educational practices. There is, of course, a great difference between making an assumption and always being able to carry it out in practice. All children on occasions, and some children on many occasions, will prove recalcitrant for different reasons, not all of which are within the teacher's sphere of influence. A child may be unwell, handicapped, emotionally disturbed because of conditions at home or quite simply in a bad temper. He and his teacher may not get on together. The tasks set him may be unsuitable, pointless or too difficult. Yet, if the basic assumption is that he is a willing learner, the results, overall, will be immeasurably better than if the opposite assumption is made.

Fourth to be rejected is a relationship between teacher and child that can be indicated, but not defined, by the word 'authoritarian'. This is a relationship in which the teacher demands the formal and automatic respect of the child *de jure*, in which he behaves always as an officer in command and in which he is always right. He may fill these roles in a friendly manner and may be quite effective as a teacher of clever children, but essentially everything is done on his terms. This teacher-child relationship is very widespread in the world and there are probably tens of thousands of teachers to whom any other relationship is inconceivable. It is not the purpose of this book to hold up such teachers to ridicule, contempt or dislike. They are what they are because they have been trained and conditioned to this way of teaching.

But it must be stated categorically that the changes described and recommended here cannot take place so long as the authoritarian teacher-child relationship persists. This is not to say that teachers must have no authority, that they must simply stand aside and be ready to help when called upon. This has been tried here and there by teachers who have not properly understood the nature of the change in relationship which is called for, and the results have been deplorable. Children need much more from their teachers than a helping hand. What that more is will be discussed in the course of this book.

Teachers who are working in systems which approximate to what has been described above as needing rejection may feel inclined to dismiss what is proposed as absurd and Utopian, or they may admire it but feel it to be too difficult to put into practice. Some may be filled with enthusiasm and desire to act upon it at once. It is hoped that the chapters which follow will provide food for thought for holders of all these opinions.

Chapter 2
Why change?

Anyone who recommends a revolutionary change in an educational system might be expected to do two things. First, he might be expected to be able to point to evils and deficiencies in the body politic which were demonstrably attributable to the system which he is condemning. In fact this can be done only in a very limited way. That there is a causal connection between, say, crime, violence, dishonesty, vice and other signs of social sickness on the one hand and the educational system on the other is little more than a conjecture. The difficulty about testing it statistically is that the variables are both numerous and correlated. This makes it likely that the results of a statistical inquiry would lend themselves to more than one interpretation; in such circumstances it is easier to assess the combined effects of the variables than their individual effects, which leaves the conclusion rather indeterminate.

A more limited pedagogical study is more possible and has in fact been undertaken.[2] It has been shown, for instance, that standards of reading in 11-year-old English children in 1964 had improved by 16 per cent on the standards of 1948. These facts are not in dispute but the interpretation of them is. Some critics have sought to show that 1948 was a 'bad' year, following a period of war-time disturbance and that some or most of the improvement was no more than a normal recovery of lost ground. The absence of reliable pre-war statistics makes this view impossible to prove or refute. In any case, the children in the sample were drawn from every kind of primary school and the results therefore prove nothing about the respective merits of traditional and progressive education.

It would certainly be possible to undertake a comparative

study of the achievements in the 3 Rs of two groups of schools, one avowedly traditional and the other avowedly progressive but even this would prove little. What would be measured, though important, would be too limited. Supposing, for example, that the traditional group scored more highly in spelling than the progressive group, it would still have to be shown (and this would involve value-judgement) that this deficiency was not compensated for by other unmeasured and possibly unmeasurable achievements such as width and quality of reading, powers of conversation and social awareness.

All that can be said in the end is that, if society is a product of the educational systems in force in the world, there is nothing to justify a particularly favourable view of those systems. And, since the great majority of them are 'traditional', there is a prima facie case for looking at an alternative.

The second thing that the upholder of revolutionary change might be expected to do is to offer convincing evidence that the changes he is recommending will produce an improvement and, it must be added, a marked improvement. The price of change is bound to be considerable and would be too heavy to pay for a marginal improvement, still more so for a doubtful one. All innovation in so complex and subtle a business as the education of children must have in it an element of faith but it should be founded on good evidence. The evidence in the present case comes from two sources, the research done in the fields of child psychology and the learning process and the experience gained over a period of years mainly in English schools.

The researches of Susan Isaacs and her co-workers showed that children work best from a situation that is familiar to them and both Tolman and Bruner have suggested that they approach learning with an expectation based on past experience and use this past experience in solving new problems. Piaget also showed that young children need to learn through the everyday and the familiar and to use this kind of learning to make a gradual advance into learning within the conventional subject fields. That is to say that the conventional skills and elementary knowledge of language and number will best be learned, not by a direct formal didactic approach but through a variety of experience and activity of a more general kind. Research also gives support to the view that children work best when they are interested and when they have some degree of choice both in what they do and when they do it.

It cannot be claimed that research has yet produced a universally acceptable or adequate theory of learning. We can watch children learning and observe within limits what they have learned and failed to learn, but most would agree that we cannot yet say exactly how it is done. The researches of Piaget and Inhelder into the stages of children's learning have thrown much light on the process and, among other things, have indicated that learning, if it is to be successful, must be enjoyable. This does not mean that it must be a continuous riot of fun or that it must be shorn of all its difficulties or relieved of all the duller moments, but simply that it is most effective when it is looked upon by the learner as a primarily enjoyable occupation.

This is not the place to summarise all the research which sheds light on the matter in hand. Its importance is not so much in its direct influence upon teaching as in the support it has, on the whole, given to teaching methods which have been evolved intuitively by gifted teachers.*

The experience on which the kind of education described in this book is founded goes back a long way in England. The abolition in 1898 of the rigid, centrally imposed Code was followed in 1905 by the publication of *The Handbook of Suggestions for the consideration of Teachers in Elementary Schools*.[3] The preface to this volume contained the following remarkable words:

> The only uniformity of practice that the Board of Education desires to see in the teaching of Public Elementary Schools is that each teacher should think for himself and work out for himself such methods of teaching as may use his powers to the best advantage and be best suited to the particular needs and conditions of the school.

This was concerned with methods. A centrally devised programme still existed. This was not abolished until 1926, but a beginning had been made in the liberation of the teacher from central control. There has thus been for sixty-nine years an opportunity for individual experiment in method and organisation and, for forty-

---

* See list of books for further reading on page 106.

eight years, in curriculum. The selection examination at 11, until recently universal, has acted as a brake and as a disincentive to experiment, but it remains true that experiment has been possible, that from the beginning some teachers took the opportunity and that, increasingly since 1945, teachers have taken the initiative in bringing about change. It has not been a question of trying out other people's programmes but of genuine personal experiment, fed by ideas and suggestions coming from a variety of sources.

It would be absurd to claim that all experiments have been successful or that no mistakes have been made. Some have made changes ill-advisedly, not from conviction or knowledge, but from a desire to be in the fashion. But, broadly speaking, the trend of change, founded upon experience in the classroom and initiated teacher-by-teacher and school-by-school, has been in the direction with which this book is concerned and it has continued because the results have been convincing. When, in 1967, the Plowden Council[4] reported on English primary education after a period of three years spent in examining it, it came out in favour of what is generally known as the progressive approach. Subsequent attempts to denigrate this approach, though they have sounded some useful warnings against the misuses based on misunderstandings, have carried little weight.

This chapter may be summarised by saying that the justification for recommending the progressive approach is that there is no evidence that the traditional one is proving so successful that it clearly ought to be retained, and that there is reasonably good evidence, based on research as well as experience, that the progressive approach is more suited to what is known of children and their development and produces better all-round results. But this statement seems to imply a polarisation which is not intended or recommended. The progressive approach has been arrived at in terms of modifying the traditional and it is probably best still to regard it in that light, rather than see the two of them as incompatibles. At the two extremes the differences are indeed very great but there is a road between and part of the aim of this book is to map that road.

A further justification of a move, drastic or moderate, is ethical in nature and, to some extent, a matter of opinion. The writer's opinion is that the progressive approach treats children and teachers as persons, as individual souls if you prefer it, to a greater extent than the traditional. It allows a greater place for love, both in the sense of the Greek *philia* and in that of *agape*, and is therefore more in harmony with the vision of human happiness which still brightens our dreams, however much it may elude our grasp.

Chapter 3
Aims of primary education

In one sense it is very easy to draw up a list of the aims of primary or any other kind of education, yet the Plowden Council,[5] when they came to consider the matter closely, found it one of the most difficult of their tasks. They consulted experts and, when they published their conclusions, were much criticised by, among others, some of the experts consulted whose views they thought they had expressed.

In a book of this kind, which is an appeal for change, something must be said about aims, however elusive they turn out to be on examination.

There are first of all certain fairly short-term pedagogical aims which can be clearly stated and which at first glance look simple. For instance: 'Children are to be taught to read, fluently and with understanding, matter suitable to their age.' This is an aim which would command universal assent. It is essential to be able to read. Reading can, save very exceptionally, only be acquired if some, often much, direct teaching is given. Reading matter must suit those who read it. Fluency and speed, in some degree, are desirable and reading without understanding is futile. The aim looks pretty watertight, yet it raises questions at every point. At what age are children to begin reading? How much can be directly taught and how much must be learned by practice and experience? What alphabet is to be used, t.o. or i.t.a?[6] What sort of reading matter is suitable? What emphasis is to be placed on phonics and on look-and-say and at what period? At what age is it reasonable to expect that this aim should be achieved? How is understanding to be defined, let alone tested? Most teachers might feel able to answer these questions to their own satisfaction but the answers would not be the same, which means that, to command wide assent, the aim must be confined to the very general 'Children must learn to read' which is self-evident and scarcely worth uttering.*

Mathematics looks even more susceptible to the formulation of aims: 'Children are to be taught to add, subtract, multiply and divide with speed and accuracy.' This can be extended to include other mathematical operations, such as measuring, fractions, the use of money, time. But why teach them mathematics at all? The day-to-day uses of the subject, though indispensable, are very limited. Would it be a sufficient aim simply to meet these uses? Almost everybody would say that it would not. What other elements then, besides the everyday ones, are to be included? For the great majority, who will never need to use or understand the workings of computers, is there any purpose in working on a binary base? Or is mathematics so interesting in itself that it should be regarded as a cultural subject? Is this to apply to all children? Could some children drop mathematics at quite an early stage? Any teacher of mathematics can make up his mind on all this, draw up a syllabus and say: 'This is what I propose to teach the children in my class.' But what has happened to the general aim? It has become no more than the banal: 'Children are to learn some mathematics.'†

We may now examine a more subtle pedagogical aim: 'Children are to learn how to think.' Does this imply that they are to be *taught* how to think and, if so, by what methods? Children can think, within limits which are very partially defined, with much success before they arrive in school and without having received any conscious or systematic teaching. By the time they leave school they can think in a more abstract way. How much of this is attributable to maturation, how much to the general experience of being in school and how much to deliberate teaching? Nobody can say with any degree of certainty. Nevertheless, the aim is an important one. On this every teacher would agree, and good teachers keep it pretty constantly in mind and do whatever they can to encourage thinking. There are many tests of a mathematical, logical or

* See Chapter 8.
† See Chapter 11.

constructional nature which demand considerable powers of thought. Familiarity and experience with these tests can lead to improved performance in tackling similar tests, but whether there is any transfer to other types of problem or to thinking in general is more than doubtful. The traditional system, with its emphasis on rote learning, on the performance of set tasks and domination by the teacher, was not well designed for the purpose. The progressive approach, with its emphasis on initiative, discovery and independence, seems more likely to provide opportunities for thought. It will not of itself ensure clear and logical thinking but it will allow it to take place if the guidance given by the teacher is well planned.

A fourth pedagogical aim has been expressed by a well-known educational philosopher as 'the initiation of children into worthwhile activities'.[7] These are rather surprisingly vague words to come from such a source but they imply something important, namely, the view that there are some fields of study which are more valuable than others and it is to these that all children ought to be introduced. The contrary view, that the intrinsic value of what is studied is unimportant and that children should study whatever interests them, has been expressed, and it is important to be clear about this issue, though it is not really a very live one.

Upon the main content of the primary school curriculum there is very wide agreement. Hardly any teacher would deny that it should include the use of the mother tongue, the literature of that tongue, mathematics, science, history and geography, music, art, craft and physical education. There can be few, if any, primary schools in which these subjects in some form or other do not figure. A second language and some kind of religious study appear in some but not all curricula. That these are the components of a good education and that it is wrong to omit any of them is common ground between traditional and progressive. There would be a difference in emphasis as between the components but upon what the components should be there would be accord. Where a more serious difference might be found would be first in what was selected for study in each field, for some selection there must obviously be whatever approach is favoured, and secondly in the ways in which the material chosen was itself selected, arranged and used. These differences will be considered in a later chapter, but for the time being we can accept the very general and indeed self-evident aim quoted at the beginning of the previous paragraph.

We come now to the moral and social aims of education. Here again there would be very general agreement that the virtues of integrity, honesty, truthfulness, consideration for others, fair play, sportsmanship perhaps, tolerance, forbearance and courtesy, to name only a few, are desirable and that schools should do what they can to encourage them. But this is little more than a pious hope. By what means are they to be encouraged? Part of the answer undoubtedly lies in the example set by the school and especially by its teachers. By living in a community in which these virtues are upheld, children will learn to respect and practise them. In such a community the rights and liberties of everyone, children and teachers, will be respected and the responsibilities of all acknowledged; there will be mutual respect between adults and children; so far as possible there will be no violence to bodies or feelings; there will be no exclusion and no second-class members.

There are schools which approximate to this ideal picture and they tend to be of the progressive rather than the traditional type. It is not that the virtues cannot exist in a rigid and formal pattern but rather that they are more likely to flourish in a more flexible one, because the flexible one depends mainly upon good human relationships for its success. If strict discipline, unquestioning obedience and domination by the teacher are taken away, something positive must be put in their place or the result will be the chaos which hostile critics are so fond of imagining. But, at whatever point on the road between old and new a school is placed, it will, intentionally or unintentionally, set an example to its pupils in the matter of morals, and there are many who believe that not only is this the most effective kind of moral training but even perhaps the only effective kind.

We must, however, consider the possibility of explicit moral training. In some countries there is a code of behaviour and time is found regularly for lessons on this. In others the pupils themselves draw up such a code and, when it has been adopted, do something to enforce it. In schools with a religious connection the moral teaching will be more or less firmly based upon a faith. In all schools there are certain moral assumptions which, however informally, are made explicit in situations as they arise. It is thus a matter on which fairly wide disagreement is liable to occur even concerning the primary stage that is here being considered and much more so concerning the secondary. This disagreement becomes more marked when we look at the question of how offenders against this code, whatever it is, are to be treated and by whom the sentence, if there is one, is to be carried out. Some educationalists set great store by the popular court—the trial of children by children—while others consider that this imposes too heavy a moral burden. Some believe that all punishments (and awards) are, if not absolutely wrong, at least confessions of failure. Others think that punishments of some kind cannot be avoided and even that they may be beneficial, not merely preventive. These disagreements will be reflected not only in the explicit moral training given but even more so in the general moral atmosphere of the school. They make it impossible at this stage to formulate the ways in which the moral aims of primary education are to be carried out.

Finally we must consider political aims. In different parts of the world these may take such varying forms as: 'To arouse in the children gratitude to the Party for providing such good education for them'; 'To arouse in the children a respect for democracy'; 'To train the children to be loyal to King and country'; 'To encourage in the children the love of all men and the desire to improve society and make it more just'; 'To help the children to understand the government and institutions of their country and thus learn to respect them'; 'To bring up the children to be God-fearing and obedient'. It is only necessary to read these aims and others like them to realise that to attain common political aims is at present a hopeless task. It must be added, however, that some of the aims listed above are incompatible with the approach with which this book is concerned. This is perhaps obvious. An approach which encourages children to think for themselves, to exercise choice, to ask questions, to co-operate, will not also encourage them to accept unexamined the society in which they live

and its institutions; nor will it encourage an unthinking icono-
clasm. The aim is to encourage a critical sensitiveness and understanding of society. Those who cannot tolerate this would do well
to reject the approach.*

* See Chapter 12.

Chapter 4
What changes?

The foregoing rationale of change may not be thought altogether satisfactory. It does not bring to the question a standard of validation which would be acceptable in, for instance, the physical sciences. This is because no methods of such validation have yet been found to exist. It is necessary to act on the weight of the evidence and this, it is suggested, favours a change towards the approach here recommended. Many would put it in much more emphatic terms than this and the remark, 'I was very doubtful when we first started but now I would *never* go back to the old methods,' is often heard. But this book is not written for the converted and I do not want to overstate the case or even to appear to do so.

We must now look at what the changes involve in practice. This will be considered under four headings but all are closely linked and one is hardly possible without the other.

A. Informality

Under this heading are discussed the physical changes that are involved. The teacher's dais and desk and the rows of children's desks disappear. Instead, there are tables and chairs grouped about the room in the most convenient way. This is a much more economical use of space. It allows free movement about the room for children and teacher and it emphasises the new relationship between them. For reasons that will become clear in the next section, it is not usually necessary to have seats for every child. The doors will often be left open and, if there is a corridor outside, the children will overflow into this and find more space for their activities. Again, if there are french windows opening on to a garden or lawn or paved area, these will be open in suitable weather and the children allowed to move outside.

All this assumes that the school building has been designed for traditional class organisation and teaching and that change in approach has to take place without any corresponding structural change in the building. The more recent school buildings in the United Kingdom, and here and there elsewhere, are not constructed on a classroom basis at all but on some kind of open plan which provides for space, for quiet and noisy, clean and dirty activities and for a maximum of free movement.

It is obvious that these physical changes in themselves will achieve nothing but chaos and uproar. Children accustomed to sit in rows and silence under the teacher's eye, to move only when given permission and to raise their hands before being allowed to speak, if suddenly let loose in a building such as has been described, would run riot. Similarly a teacher whose experience of control had been limited to the old formal discipline would be at a total loss if confronted with a free and fluid situation. Both teacher and children have to learn to use it. How this may be done will be discussed later. Meanwhile the sceptical reader is asked to take it on trust that neither chaos nor uproar is, or ought to be, the consequence of informality and that a much better discipline can be established by means of it, with far less of the waste of time and energy that is too often the characteristic of the formal classroom.

The disposition not only of furniture but of teaching and learning materials will also be quite different in the informal building. What the children need, such as books, maps, writing materials, apparatus, tools, brushes and paint, will be immediately available to them instead of being handed out by the teacher or under his supervision. There will thus be no waiting at the beginning and end of a lesson while the books are given out or collected. This does not mean that the entire material resources of the school will be simultaneously available to all its pupils. What it does mean is that the teacher will see to it that, at any given time, the materials likely to be needed by the children (and this may involve a very wide range) will be available without any ado. It will also mean that he himself must have ready to hand what he is going to need for teaching purposes. This also may involve a wide range because, as will be shown later, he will often, though not always, be teaching individuals and small groups rather than the class as a whole. His own resourcefulness and ability to organise his work efficiently will be much more severely tested than in formal conditions, and his preparation will have to be no less thorough, however much use he may, and indeed is bound to, make of improvisation in the course of the day.

B. Choice

It is implicit in all section A that the children will have a wide freedom of choice in what they do and when they do it. This is nearly always a great stumbling block to the unconverted. 'How on earth,' they ask, 'can you ensure that the children do not always choose what is easy and exciting? How can you ensure that they learn systematically and thoroughly? How can you keep track of what they have learned?' These, of course, are crucial questions. If all that is happening is that the children are having an interesting and enjoyable time, if they are just happily occupied, then the system is a failure. Let it be said at once that this can and sometimes does happen. Where the change is made by teachers who do not properly understand either the nature or the vital importance of the teacher's place and part in the process, then learning is limited and disorganised and standards of achievement low.

The main problems of carrying out the change will be considered later but the questions posed in the last paragraph can be answered immediately. The children's choice is not completely unfettered. It must be made within a structure or scheme of which the children may be only partially aware but which must be very clear in the teacher's mind. This may be effected by a system of assignments and records. The assignment may be a general one. Each child will be expected to devote a certain amount of time to, say, formal mathematics (i.e. practice), written work, reading, his individual or group project and so forth, and to cover a reasonable amount of ground during a week or month. Within this time he will be free to choose what he is going to do. There will be other times when he may have no choice at all, when the teacher will be in complete charge of what is going on, as for example in PE or music, though in both of these subjects there will be many opportunities for free choice, so to speak, internally. That is to say that, although a whole class may be doing PE or music simultaneously under the teacher's direction, there will be a choice of activities in the former and perhaps of instruments in the latter. The essence of this method is that the main motivation should be interest, with coercion reduced to the lowest possible limit.

The general assignment will be reinforced by some degree of individual assignment. The teacher, moving about the class, will be constantly discussing with individuals and groups what they are doing and this will lead to suggestions or requirements as to what they should do next, either as a supplement, a development, a reinforcement or a corrective. The children themselves will contribute suggestions and ask questions and sometimes the conclusion will be: 'Well, try it out and see what happens' or 'I think that would be too difficult for you just at present. Instead I should try this.'

Clearly such a system demands some well thought-out and carefully kept records. The teacher must know what each child has done and learned and whether his progress is satisfactory. This task will be greatly simplified and lightened if each child keeps a folder of his work—written English, mathematics, art—at which the teacher may look at any time and see almost at a glance how he is doing.

The teacher must also have a record of his own. Such records and, indeed, the whole business of keeping track of the children vary a great deal. A loose-leaf notebook, with a page or pages for each child, in which the teacher writes down from day to day any information that is relevant, is favoured by many. There are printed records with assessment scales and all the rest of the elaborate devices thought up by experts but, in the United Kingdom at least, these are seldom used because they involve a disproportionate amount of time with a minimum return. In one excellent English school, run on very free lines, the headmistress, when asked what she did about keeping track of the children, said: 'Well, this is a fairly small school. The staff are mostly experienced and have been here for some time. We are constantly discussing the children and comparing notes. We don't have staff meetings as such because a sort of informal staff meeting is going on the whole time.' The headmaster of another equally good school, run on even freer lines, said: 'The staff must meet in my room for half an hour every day at lunch-time and once a week after school for perhaps two hours. This is absolutely essential in a school run on these lines if we are to keep track of each child. We must share our experience and problems and pool our knowledge.' This is clear evidence that different procedures suit different people and that head teachers in England have power of decision and independence from higher authority.

C. Initiative

A good deal about initiative has been implicit in the previous section. Choice and initiative are closely connected—but there are certain important points that need emphasising and these are best dealt with under the latter heading.

The initiative of the individual child is encouraged far beyond the making of choices as between material or activities provided by the school. That is to say, if a child comes to the teacher and says, 'My parents took me to Stonehenge last week-end and I should like to study it further' (or words to that effect), he will not be told, 'You can't, it's not in the programme' or 'You can't' (with the unspoken excuse: 'I don't know anything about it myself'). Nor, on the other hand, will the teacher say: 'Splendid! Go ahead and good luck.' She may say: 'Well, I don't think we have any books about Stonehenge (or whatever it may be) in the school. Have you any yourself? I'll inquire at the Public Library or you can and then we'll see. You can't manage much without books but, of course, you'll have to go to Stonehenge again when you've read them. Perhaps you'll want to make a scale model and, in any case, you'll have to do some measurements. Is there anyone else you know who is interested?' In other words, the child's initiative is taken seriously and supported and at the same time he is made to realise that what he proposes will involve systematic study and work. The outcome may be a group or a class project or it may remain individual. At all points the child will be encouraged to work on his own and with others and at the end to produce something—a book illustrated with drawings and photographs perhaps—which is in itself a good piece of work.

The example given is one of an extended initiative but there are many occasions when initiative may be shown on a smaller scale. It may be simply a piece of information or something found and brought to school, a dead bird, a caterpillar, an odd-shaped stone, or a request for information or a suggestion. It will *never* be scorned or just rejected but always received with gratitude, taken seriously and, where possible, used, so that the children's general initiative is encouraged; they are made to feel that they have a contribution to make and are helped to look critically at their own efforts.

The teacher himself must have initiative. If he does not, he cannot give it to the children. He must be free to act on what a situation demands, to vary any plans he has made or has had made for him, to extend the time allowed for any particular activity, to go outside the school for material and support—in short, to act like a free person and not like a transmitter. Finally he must not be frustrated in doing this by the demands of an examination designed for a very different kind of school.

D. Discovery

'I hear and I forget, I see and I remember, I do and I understand.' This Chinese proverb is often used as a kind of thumbnail justification of what are sometimes called 'discovery methods' in the primary school. With it may be contrasted the following observations by Professor B. F. Skinner: 'The school of experience is no school at all, not because no one learns in it but because no one teaches. Teaching is the expedition of learning; a person who is taught learns more quickly than one who is not.'[8] This could be, and has been used as, a sort of text to a sermon directed against discovery methods. Both sayings are incomplete in that the first seems to assume that learning takes place without any teaching. It can and often does but not all the time. The second seems to assume that to withold teaching is to slow up the process of learning and this is patently untrue. Both sayings illustrate the danger of polarity in educational argument and of dogmatic utterance. Both underestimate the complexity of learning.

What changes?

If a child of six is given, say, a glass container three-quarters full of water, a piece of wood and a number of pebbles, he will, more or less quickly, discover the fact that the wood floats and the pebbles do not, the fact that, if the pebbles are put into the water, the level of the surface rises, and the fact that, if the pebbles are taken out, the water on them in due course disappears. Moreover, he finds that these events are invariable: they happen every time he performs the operations. He could, of course, be told these facts by a teacher and they could be demonstrated to him. This would initially take much less time. Alternatively, the child could make this discovery for himself and the teacher could then, by a mixture of questions and statements, help him to extend the discovery and generalise from the particular. The teacher could, for example, say: 'Find what other things sink and float in water.' Later on the child would be helped to think out why some things float and others sink. Again, the teacher could say: 'How long do the pebbles take to dry? Do they always take the same time? Can you think of any way to hurry up or slow down the process?' Later again the child could be helped to discover the relationship between the volume of the pebbles and the displacement of the water and how to use the latter to measure the former. The delight of finding out for oneself is never lost in this way of learning, but the teacher is intervening both to expedite the process and to systematise what is learned.

In *Mathematics in the Primary School*[9] a story is told of a 10-year-old boy who asked his teacher: 'Why do bees use hexagons in building their honeycombs?' The teacher replied: 'Go and find out for yourself.' The boy experimented with triangles and squares and found that, with a given perimeter, the hexagon encloses more space than either. He also discovered that circles are better still but that they do not fit and decided that the hexagon was the most economical shape to use. Was this time wasted or time well spent? Obviously the boy could not have done what he was told to do (i.e. find out himself) without previous experience of the same kind, and training in how to set about solving problems. Had he been taught formally, simply to carry out set operations, he would have been at a total loss, if confronted with such a demand, because, unless he was a very exceptional person, he could not have developed the independence from textbook and teacher (old style) that is necessary to meet it.

How vital the teacher's role is may be illustrated by a personal experience. Many years ago I came across an elderly hermit who lived in a hut in a wood in North Wales. He turned out to be a keen bird-watcher and I had an enjoyable talk with him about the birds that he had seen. He showed himself to be a very acute and accurate observer but he told me that cuckoos turned into hawks in the winter. This was widely believed in seventeenth-century England before much was known about migration. The hermit was illiterate. He had learned solely in the school of experience and was unable to learn from books and thus share the experience of others. This is the situation imagined by Professor Skinner and he is entirely right in what he says about it. But it is not one that I have ever found in a British primary school. Learning by experience and discovery is interwoven at every point with the influence of the teacher mediated in a variety of ways. Didactic instruction is a part of teaching but only a part. The interaction between the teacher's mind and the child's mind is not simply a plain stimulus-response pattern but an exchange by means of question and answer, of discussion, of shared interest and pleasure, of information coming from both sides, of co-operation and independence. This interaction cannot be expressed as a formula, but examples of it will be described in a later chapter.

E. Integration

A good deal has already been said about integration, which may be described as a variety of practices and devices, all of which break up the subdivisions of the time-table and the curriculum characteristic of the traditional approach, and rearrange both in a more organic fashion. It is interesting that this is also being done at the Open University[10] and that the same kind of criticism is directed to the practice at both primary and higher levels.

The basis of the criticism at both levels is that integration is liable to lead to superficiality, to a nodding acquaintance with a variety of topics, to a failure to accept and benefit from the essential disciplines. There is an implication in this view that, at any rate in the primary school, the traditional system nurtured these disciplines, that children taught by it learned in depth and acquired the habits of the scholar. Nothing could be further from the truth. The great majority of the products of popular education in the past knew nothing in depth and nothing of scholarship. These were the virtues or attributes of the chosen few.

Will integration make things worse or better? The answer must depend in this, as in everything else, upon the teacher. If the teacher's knowledge and scholarship are deficient, he will never, whatever programme or method he uses, teach his children to know thoroughly or to work accurately because he will have no experience himself of thoroughness or accuracy. No programme, however well devised, can rescue him from this plight. It is not necessary for him to know thoroughly everything with which his teaching is concerned. What is essential is that he must know something in sufficient depth for him to be able to recognise superficiality when he sees it and to recognise and emulate scholarship. If he can do this, integration will hold no dangers for him or his children. He will help them to explore the riches of their culture and environment, crossing boundaries freely and using any references and connections which prove fruitful. What this means in terms of classroom practice will be described in the next chapter.

Chapter 5
In the classroom

At this point it seems advisable to describe some actual classroom situations which exhibit the changes in practice. Since some educational writers who prefer to regard education primarily as a science rather than an art dismiss such description as 'anecdotalism', it may be as well to begin by saying what it can and cannot do.

It cannot provide a model. Models in education are of very limited application for, as soon as they begin to be used, they are adapted, even in the most rigid systems, and become not models but examples. It cannot provide a guarantee or a proof. That is, it cannot declare, 'If you do as this teacher does, it will be a success' or 'If this practice were to become universal, the system would be a success'. On the other hand, it can do much. It can stimulate thought, it can inspire and, if enough teachers think about it and are inspired by it, it can be an agent of change. Instances of success are always worth hearing about. Instances of failure, too, can be of great usefulness; but, when they take the form of general accusations based on particular instances unsupported by sound evidence, they seldom prove anything more than that some people do silly things some of the time. In other words, a single success is interesting, and a single failure proves nothing.

The situations that I am going to describe are all genuine and occurred in schools of which I have personal knowledge. There is nothing imaginary or composite about them. Each illustrates, in varying degrees, the putting into practice of informality, choice, initiative, discovery and integration, and each illustrates the part played by teachers in the process.

A. The playwrights

The school was for boys only and stood in a working-class area in a great industrial city. The class was IIIB, that is, the lower stream in the third year of a junior school. With two exceptions the boys were below average IQ for their age and the great majority came from homes which were, economically speaking, poor, and culturally deficient. Absenteeism was high and attendance in the juvenile courts frequent. The young woman teacher who, as a new and quite inexperienced member of the staff, was given the task of coping with this collection of young human beings described the work they were doing in these words: 'All this work was stereotyped, orthodox and uninspiring. It was imposed from above. It taught the boys what it was supposed they ought to learn, without reference to their natural reactions or inclinations. It allowed no scope for their own initiative; it kept them passive when they should have been active, dull when they should have been enthusiastic, barren when they should have been creative. Their natural impulses were stifled and found their outlet in restless behaviour and talkativeness, in-attention and boredom.'

The boys responded almost at once to the charm and sympathy of their new teacher. The crucial moment occurred when she found on her desk a letter which ran as follows: 'Theanks for lrnine me leson and sums.' The writer was Albert, 8 years 4 months old, with an IQ of 79·3. 'This,' said the teacher, 'was a golden opportunity not to be lost.' She wrote a reply, put it in an envelope and placed it on Albert's desk. The result was that all the other boys wanted letters too and there began an enthusiastic exchange of letters between teacher and children on every conceivable subject. Writing was no longer a set exercise but a means of communication with an incentive.

At an early stage in the proceedings the boys decided that there ought to be a letter-box in which the letters could be posted. An old cardboard box was used for a few days, after which one of them said, 'Let's make a real letter-box.' There was a real letter-box just down the road. Nowadays there would be no difficulty about going out during school hours to look at it but this was 1943 and it had to be done after school hours. The story continues in the teacher's own words:

From the surge of volunteers four were chosen and at the conclusion of afternoon school Arnold, Teddy, Neville, George and a panting teacher scurried up the street and round the corner to the nearby post-box. The post-box was carefully measured and the measurements checked and recorded. Arnold, commissioned to write down the measurements, actually felt for the first time in his school career an active need to be able to speak the words he required. But George, reserved and taciturn as always, automatically stood by with his hands in his pockets until, at a judicious suggestion that he should hold one end of the tape measure, he was drawn into the activity. Indeed, as one grew to understand George better one realised that, in spite of his apparent lethargy, he keenly desired 'to be in things' but his emotions were always suppressed and his spontaneous reactions inhibited.

Every sentence in that paragraph is revealing.

That was the beginning. By the end of the year the boys had written, collectively, a play in four scenes called *The Sword in the Anvil*, founded on an Arthurian legend. They had constructed the scenery, costumes and properties, after research in books concerning swords, helmets and armour, and they had staged the play to a cramped audience of mothers and of baby brothers and visitors, a gathering in which the adult members began watching in a spirit of toleration and ended by being impressed. The standard of writing generally improved steadily throughout the year because there was a new-born desire to write. The same thing happened with reading, arithmetic and speech. 'It was impossible to deny,' writes the teacher, 'that very appreciable strides had been made in the field of the 3 Rs, and equally impossible to believe that such improvements would have emerged had the old barren methods of conscientious plodding by a despairing teacher been retained for another twelve months. Not only was it proved that these intellectual subjects could be taught by less orthodox means, but it was clearly demonstrated that they could be thus taught with greater success.'

This particular experiment was written up in detail by the teacher and the claims she makes are well supported in her account by facts and figures. The account, published under the title of *Experiments with a Backward Class* by Elizabeth Taylor,[11] is unfortunately out of print. The saddest and most incredible sentences in it are these: 'The story of IIIB was now ended and the boys passed on to the next standard [this term survived long after 1926 when standards were abolished]. They returned once more to the old régime—to the collective class instruction, the dictated syllabus, the formal time-table, and the classroom restrictions of former times.' It is interesting that the headmaster was quite unaware of what was going on in IIIB, except that they were no longer giving trouble, until he was invited to see the play, by which he was considerably startled and impressed. It is encouraging to hear that 'the experience of IIIB left its mark upon them so that, at a later date, it was possible for a member of the staff to pick out, mainly by his attitude, a boy who had come under the influence of "that year".'

B. The gardeners

The school was rural and near the sea, in a climatic zone more equable than that of most of the British Isles. It stood on an ample site on the outskirts of a small port. It included boys and girls, with an age range of 7 to 13. The area at the time of which I write was obsessed, more than most, by the importance of obtaining good results in the secondary school selection examination; and work, even in the infants' schools, was much influenced by this, with a heavy emphasis on measurable performance in the 3 Rs. Fortunately, in contrast, a strong musical tradition led to a reasonable amount of time and trouble being devoted to singing and dancing, both of which reached a high standard. The school, when a new headmaster took it over, was characteristic of the area. His own passion was for gardening. This was a recognised school subject in the secondary schools of the area and was practised in a rather half-hearted way in some of the primary schools. This particular school at the time had not been re-organised and contained children of both primary and secondary age.

The school garden occupied a considerable portion of the site and gradually more and more of the work began to be centred on it. The science, for instance, included studies and recordings of germination, pollination, propagation, soil analysis, soil temperature, rainfall, wind velocity and direction and sunshine, all of which could be undertaken on the school site. Records were kept of weeds, wild birds and some insects which occurred on the school site and these were compared with the species of flora, birds and insects to be found a short distance away on the sea cliffs. Handicraft for the older boys involved the making of wheel-barrows, spade handles, frames and ladders, all needed for the garden. The produce of the kitchen garden and the school poultry shed was marketed and the children kept all the accounts and could buy a limited number of shares in this enterprise from which they received a dividend. The counting, weighing, pricing and marketing of the produce and the distribution of dividends as well as the measurements and calculations involved in the horticultural processes provided most of the opportunities for applied mathematics.

Thus it was that all the science and handicraft, much of the mathematics, a good deal of the written English and some of the reading and the use of books were given an immediacy and a focus by the centre of interest, which was the garden. The garden was also used as a starting point and a point of reference in some of the historical and geographical work which was concerned, though not exclusively, with food supply and with the origins and needs of human settlements.

This scheme is open to criticism. It may be objected that it was the headmaster's hobby rather than the children's interest or choice which formed the centre; that, though gardening is a rich and a fundamental source of human knowledge, it dominated this school too much and for too long; that there was at least a danger of leaving out altogether or of treating as of secondary importance literature and creative writing. All these objections have substance but it must be remembered that what is described occurred in 1938 when the idea of integration was unexplored and almost unknown and that it represented an early and by no means unsuccessful attempt to do what many teachers are now doing much better. The school, as I recall it after a third of a century, had about it a liveliness and purposefulness rare in those days and its achievements in terms of examination results were considerable. The death of the headmaster and the reorganisation of the school early in the war brought the experiment to an end.

C. The archaeologists

The school was a small two-class place in an agricultural village. It had been run for years on very traditional lines. When at last the old headmistress retired and continued to live in the village it was under her disapproving eye that the new young headmaster and his wife had to work.

He was a keen amateur archaeologist and he soon discovered that the rough meadow on the other side of the playground wall was the site of the medieval village. He asked the children whether they would like to excavate the site and, after school on summer evenings, a gang of volunteers began on the task. As the foundations were uncovered and various artifacts came to light the children asked questions and a considerable collection of books on archaeology, history, architecture and rural craftsmanship was borrowed from the County Library. What had begun as a spare-time occupation was now part of the school work. The foundations had to be measured, charted and illustrated and their construction noted and recorded; the artifacts had to be identified, their purposes investigated and all the details written up. All the children in the upper class, with an age range of 8 to 10, took part.

When this project was well under way word of it reached the Ancient Buildings department of the Ministry of Works who, much alarmed at the thought of 'a bunch of kids', as they put it, digging up a medieval site, sent an inspector to investigate. The inspector reported that the work was a model and could hardly have been done better by professionals.

In due course the work was completed and the site covered up. By now the school was a very different place and the children willingly turned their attention to other aspects of their environment, fauna, flora, buildings, farms, which they treated in the same way. It was during this period that I visited the school. I had scarcely entered the room when a boy of 10 or so came up to me and said in a friendly tone and quite unprompted: 'Would you like to see what I am doing?' We walked across the room and he showed me some obsolete farm tools which he had collected. He was finding out their names and uses, drawing pictures of them and writing up particulars in a notebook. While I was looking at all this he said: 'The trouble about this school is that there is not enough time to do all we want to. We're trying to get Mr X to start a night school so that we can get on with our work in the evenings.' The other children were all equally busy, some on similar tasks, some reading or writing, some doing mathematics. The headmaster told me: 'I expect the children to spend a reasonable amount of time every week on the more traditional kind of work, mathematical practice, composition and so on but it is largely left to them when they do it.' A close inspection of their work showed that, by any standard, it was good—there was no shoddy, careless or untidy work but a high standard of neatness and accuracy.

Some time before my visit the headmaster had been invited to a two-day conference of teachers in the county town. He was unable to obtain a substitute, or 'supply teacher' as it is called in England, and he decided to leave his class without a teacher, apart from the general supervision of his wife who, in a separate room, was in charge of the infants. 'What happened?' I asked him. 'Well,' he said, 'they'd done a fair two days' work when I returned.'

In some ways this headmaster had an easy job. The number of children was small though their age-range was wide. They were country children, quiet and well disciplined at home and they all lived within easy reach of the school. Nevertheless, to have transformed in two years a teacher-dominated formal school into one in which informality, choice, initiative, discovery and integration were all characteristics, in which work was taken seriously and in which the virtues of accuracy and good presentation were preserved was a considerable achievement.

D. The explorers

The school was in a small industrial town with a local industry that went back to medieval times. The building was old and inconvenient for its two hundred children. Like others in the area the school had been run on traditional lines until a new headmaster took over. What I am going to describe is the work done one year by the 10-year-old children.

The town is on the slopes of a valley and the work of the

class was centred on this valley and the river that flowed in it. The whole was studied in its geographical aspect from river source to out-fall in a larger river and in its aspect as a habitat for plants and creatures. It was studied historically from the earliest human settlements at fords to later existing towns and villages, with their bridges and markets and the roads connecting them. Many visits were paid to different parts of the river and careful field studies undertaken. All the children in the class took part and all had to pay attention to all the aspects. But provision was made for individual interests and the children were able to follow these up in more detailed studies. Moreover, much emphasis was laid on enjoying the beauty of the valley and much poetry was inspired by it and written by the children, while others painted or modelled what attracted them.

It was this school which, on another occasion, weighed the parish church. This building is one of much beauty and magnificence, one of the many limestone churches characteristic of the escarpment which traverses England from Dorset to Lincolnshire. During a visit paid to it to study its architecture, one boy asked how the builders had managed to raise such large and heavy blocks of stone to such a height and this started off a discussion which developed into a study of the mechanics of the problem. During this a child said: 'I wonder how much it all weighs.' Encouraged by their teacher, the children decided to find out. This involved seeking the assistance of some local stone-masons, the actual weighing of limestone blocks of known dimensions, the allowance for difference in density between the two kinds of limestone used in the building and a great many very complex measurements, estimates and calculations before a figure which satisfied both teacher and children as being approximately correct was arrived at.

It will be apparent that there were no difficulties at this school concerned with travel. Some of the visits were to places as much as 15 miles distant and required the provision of transport. They involved absences from school of several hours and this could not have been fitted in with a normal time-table. In fact, the headmaster was free to make any arrangements he saw fit subject to a general agreement with his Local Education

Authority.[12] In this school too the measurable standards of achievement were perfectly satisfactory.

E. The quiet children

The school was in a village on the outskirts of a large industrial and university city. The green fields which once separated them had been almost swallowed up and the village had developed into a dormitory with a wide range of social classes in its population. The old village school had had to be replaced by a building for three hundred children. An enlightened Local Education Authority appointed the new headmaster before the school was built and he had a lot of say in the design and lay-out of the building, which was on an open plan with a variety of spaces large and small.

Of the five schools mentioned in this chapter this one is the most difficult to describe. A visitor might walk in at most times of the day and find the children distributed about the building and grounds apparently under no sort of control at all. The teachers, he would notice, were among them, moving from child to child, group to group and from one part of the building to another. Having recovered from the shock of seeing this apparently almost total anarchy, he would notice the extraordinary absence of noise. With no ban on conversation the children in this school are surprisingly quiet and the only explanation of this is that they are busy. They do talk to each other and to their teachers but there is none of the noisiness that some would expect and some tolerate under the mistaken impression that, if children are happy, they are noisy.

Once or twice a day the teachers gather together the group for which they are responsible (and each group includes the full age range of this school, 5 to 9) and discuss with them what they are going to do or have done. The age structure of these groups means that there cannot be teaching sessions in the ordinary sense of that word. Teaching, in that sense, is done individually or in small groups, as the need arises, but in a less specific way it goes on all the time.

The children can choose what they are going to do at any given moment but the choice is not unlimited. It is regulated by what the teachers make available. In mathematics, for instance, the material set out in one week may be entirely concerned with weighing and the calculations and computations connected with it. The teachers will see to it that the children spend enough time on this and will try to ensure that before the material is changed its use has been mastered.

Once a day the whole school meets together for an assembly which may include some singing, some listening to music, some reading from the Bible or some other book and a short talk by the headmaster. The 'hall' in which this assembly takes place is the biggest open space in the building. It is beautifully furnished and has an atmosphere rather more like that of a church than, like many school halls, of a gymnasium. It is mainly used for quiet activities.

This school has already been referred to briefly in Chapter 4 Section B, when it was said that an extremely careful system of planning and records was used in it. If this were not done, a child's progress could easily be hampered and his development checked without this being noticed for a considerable time. Yet there is something else, over and above this, going on all the time. The system allows the personality of each child not only to develop but to show itself, and this makes it much easier for the teachers to keep track of individuals than a system of formal class teaching in which personalities are at a discount. An illustration may enforce this point. I have a garden of nearly an acre containing hundreds of plants, shrubs and trees of perhaps three hundred different varieties. Sitting indoors I can recall not only nearly all of them and the positions they occupy but their state of growth. Yet I do not spend an enormous amount of my time in the garden, far less than a teacher does in school, nor do I make any systematic attempt to memorise them. Something like this process goes on in the mind of a good teacher. It is not such an extraordinary feat as it sounds.

This school probably represents the extreme limit of experiment to be found so far in English primary schools. The headmaster and staff are neither dogmatic nor self-satisfied. They devote much time to a critical examination of what they are doing, constantly looking for weakness and for possible improvements. To visit the school is a heartening experience for here is not only change but, beyond any question, a change for the better.

Chapter 6
Results

Some readers may find the descriptions in the previous chapter sufficiently convincing to justify the claim made for change and a more or less cautious move in the direction indicated. There will be others who retain lingering or insistent doubts. Such doubts may arise simply from a deep-seated unwillingness or inability to entertain new ideas but they may also be prompted by an honourable concern for the welfare of children. It seems advisable, therefore, to devote a chapter entirely to the consideration of results.

The difficulty of formulating aims described in Chapter 3 is, inevitably, exactly matched by that of assessing results. If you are not sure where you are going, how can you tell whether you have got there? Nevertheless, all teachers think in terms of the results they have obtained or failed to obtain and the easiest kind of result by which a teacher can measure his effectiveness is success in examinations. 'Seventy-five per cent of the children passed the selection exam. This was 22 per cent above the county average'; 'All but one of the children obtained more than three O levels'; 'We have won more scholarships at the university than any other school of our size.' Such claims are frequently heard. They are not meaningless or ill-founded. But they raise questions which need answering before we can join in the applause. The questions are of three kinds:

1 What was the calibre of the successful students?
Obviously a school which, from environmental or other circumstances, draws its children from a favoured social background has a better chance of achieving success than one in a slum area.

It may be that the results when scrutinised are less good than they appear, or even less good than might be reasonably expected. Obviously, too, a school which scores a very small number of successes may be doing better than might have been predicted on the basis of its catchment area and the economic conditions found there.

2 *What price is being paid for the success achieved?*

The answer to this question may be 'none' but it is a question that must be pressed home. The price may be paid by the successful students or by the unsuccessful. The former may achieve success by an excessive concentration upon the examination at the expense of important educational experiences. The latter may be sacrificed to the interests of the former, because the 'bright' children are put in the charge of the 'best' teachers or because the organisation of the school involves a low expectation of their performance.

3 *What is the examination testing?*

It may be assumed that public examinations are carefully devised and marked. But they are not divinely inspired and they may force upon teachers a range of subject-matter or a type of questioning which is contrary to what they believe is best for the children. They may give excessive weight to memorisation of facts or to mechanical operations or to facility in writing. They may punish the slow too much. They may, in fact, be very imperfect measuring instruments and success in them may be correspondingly misleading.

All this may be admitted but, if the children are going to be subjected to a public examination, success in which will affect their prospects, no teacher can conscientiously ignore it. In England where, until recently, all children in the maintained schools had to sit for a selection examination at the age of ten, this issue was a very live one in the 1940s and '50s. Some teachers slavishly prepared for the examination without disguise and rejected any innovation which looked as if it might interfere with this enterprise. Some pinned their faith to the new methods in which they believed, arguing that the far better training in thinking and the wider and deeper interest involved in them would actually enhance the children's performance even in the most unenlightened examination. The majority were somewhere in between and most of those who had accepted the new approach took some steps, as the date of the examination drew near, to prepare the children specifically for it.

No very conclusive evidence emerged from all this. There were too many variables in it. The selection examination was not a national one but differed in each Local Education Authority area. Further, educational opinion was moving against selection by whatever method and, rather more slowly, towards the innovations described in this book. All that can be said with confidence is that no evidence came to light that schools which were, on the whole, progressive rather than traditional lost anything thereby in the way of examination success.

Since that time there has been a great development of progressive methods. Many schools have abandoned classification by ability and some classification by age, and the spread of re-organisation of secondary schools has brought the process of selection by examination to an end in many areas. No reliable information on a national scale is available. There is, however, increasing co-operation and consultation between primary schools and the secondary schools to which their children go, and this dialogue between equals is leading to a better understanding by each of the needs and methods of the other.

This brings into focus a point that has been implicit in previous chapters and now needs to be made explicit. Whatever method is adopted will not suit all children equally but, unless it is patently absurd, it is likely to suit some or, anyhow, to appear to do so. At the school described in Chapter 5 under the sub-heading 'The quiet children', it was found that the most highly intelligent seemed to require a rather more formal and structured kind of learning than the rest. They were more aware of adult attitudes towards knowledge and the ways in which knowledge is classified and they wanted this to be reflected in their own work. It was part of the excellence of this school that this need came to light, that it was possible to make provision for it and that this was actually done. In a very rigid authoritarian school it is probable that a proportion of the children would adapt successfully to the demands made upon them, but such a school could not, by its very nature, make adaptations to the needs of the others. The researches of the Grants in California[13] into the responses of delinquent boys to various kinds of treatment showed that the least mature and most egocentric boys responded better to a strict, unsympathetic type of treatment than to a liberal, humane, friendly one, but this finding needs very careful interpretation. The former type of treatment may well have been re-enforcing at a deeper level the deficiencies of character which it appeared to be correcting. At the earlier junior school stage there is a better chance of correction and care, and a system which is sufficiently flexible to provide for the majority, if not all, has a far better possibility of all-round success than one which is rigid.

Flexibility *can* degenerate into chaos. A school is not only an assembly of individuals. It is also a community and there must be some kind of concordat, involving all its members, about how it is conducted. Nevertheless, the degree of flexibility that is possible in a good school, the extent to which the needs of each individual can be provided for, is very much greater than many would suppose. If success in examinations is a less illuminating result than many think, are there any results which are measurable and are capable of correlation with the traditional and the progressive approaches? An inspector might decide to look at the handwriting, neatness and lay-out of the children's written work and, though these are not absolutes, his conclusions would be likely to receive general agreement. He would be able to say, without fear of contradiction, that the majority or the great majority of the children wrote clearly or tidily or pleasantly or in a slovenly fashion and, if he knew his job, he would base his judgement upon a reasonable expectation of their capabilities. He would not, for instance, expect 6-year-olds to write like 10-year-olds. The question that seems to need an answer is whether he is more likely to find a good standard in a traditional or in a progressive school or, more particularly, whether progressive methods can preserve the high standards of neatness and good handwriting that are supposedly found in traditional ones.

About this there are three things to be said. First, the standards of neatness and handwriting in traditional schools varied and still vary from good to bad. There is no guarantee of them in any school. They are achieved by good teaching. Secondly, it would be better to use the word 'appropriate' rather than 'good'. It was not unusual in traditional schools to find a high standard of neatness and presentation in the 'show' book and nothing but a ghastly mess in the 'rough' books. What is needed, surely, is a standard appropriate to the work which is being done. Few adults adopt identical standards in personal diaries and in letters of importance, but the contrast should not be too great. Rough work must be legible. Important letters must not take all day. Thirdly, the quantity of written work done in progressive schools is so much greater than that in traditional schools that there is a tendency for the handwriting to deteriorate, sometimes to the point of illegibility. Each teacher must decide what he will tolerate and how much work and of what kind justifies an insistence upon high standards. Slovenly, careless work should never be acceptable, but it must always be remembered that what is unacceptable from one child as being below his best may represent a maximum of effort in another. The teacher, who alone knows every child in his class, must be the judge and must exercise his judgement.

This simple example provides a key to the problem of results. The virtues of hard work, accuracy, tidiness, carefulness and punctuality, often associated with the traditional school, are real virtues and the progressive school does not reject them or, if it does, is betraying the cause that it claims to uphold. It does, however, treat them as relatives and not absolutes. Moreover, it considers other virtues as well, some of which were neglected in some of the traditional schools—happiness, curiosity, co-operation, to mention only three—and tries to take into account the whole nature of children and to look for results over the whole. It thus has a much more difficult task to perform than the traditional school and a much more interesting and important one.

Chapter 7
Making a start

Teachers who have been stimulated or impressed by the accounts of the five schools in Chapter 5 may already have formed some ideas as to how they would start to make a change themselves. But these accounts are, and were intended to be, mainly inspirational. In this chapter something of the methodology is discussed.

The Project as an educational device has been with us for a great many years. It was constantly referred to in educational discussion forty years ago and is now looked upon as being a little old-fashioned. Yet all the innovations discussed in this book, by whatever name anyone calls them, are little more than developments and amplifications of the Project. The Project Method involves devoting a little, some, most or all of your time over a period, which might be a few days or a year, to work and study which revolve around a particular topic. It is no guarantee of success and has often been misunderstood and misused. Many years ago a book of projects was published, one for each week of the year with directions as to how to proceed, and even nowadays, in a more sophisticated form, some programmed learning is making the same mistake. To allow someone else to choose and plan one's project for one is to throw away half its point, most of its usefulness and all its enjoyment.

In discussing the Project as a means of starting the kind of primary education here advocated I am going to be rather more dogmatic or, at any rate, precise than I have been hitherto. I want to offer some very clear advice to readers, who having read so far, may feel in need of it.

Choice The choice of topic should be in the control of the teacher but made in consultation with the children. It is assumed here that the latter are organised in classes on the traditional principle.

Nature The topic must be of sufficient inherent richness and variety to be worth study. This needs a little consideration. It is true that almost any topic is capable of proliferating to almost any extent. The fly on the window pane could lead into studies of the spread of disease, the development of flight, the classification of insects, the pollination of plants, and these again into epidemics, powered flight, the Linnaean system and human reproduction. The fly in that case has been little more than a starting point. It cannot in any sense be said to include what follows and to proceed in that sort of way is to encourage tangential thinking and superficiality. There is a place for both but not too large a place.

Contrast with the fly a topic such as 'Our Village' or 'Our Town'. This has a limited outline which children can understand and whatever proliferates from it can be related back to it. The diagram below illustrates this. It is of a kind which can usefully be constructed at the very beginning of the undertaking and be discussed with the children. On examination it will be seen that cross-connections can be made between many of the topics which are on the branches that radiate out from the main topic. Even if the main topic is chosen by the teacher, the opportunities for individual choice and co-operation and team work are very numerous.

First-hand experience A good project will always involve first-hand experience, fieldwork and discovery. It gives the children the experiences of 'seeing for themselves', of questioning 'the people on the spot', of finding out how to find out. In countries with a highly developed literate culture this is of great importance to offset the notion that all knowledge is found in books. In countries where there is still a mainly oral tradition it will be the principal means of learning.

School B in Chapter 5 managed to run a project, successful in many respects, which hardly required any activity outside the school site. This is exceptional. The great majority of projects demand some outside work, though not necessarily at any great distance from the school building.

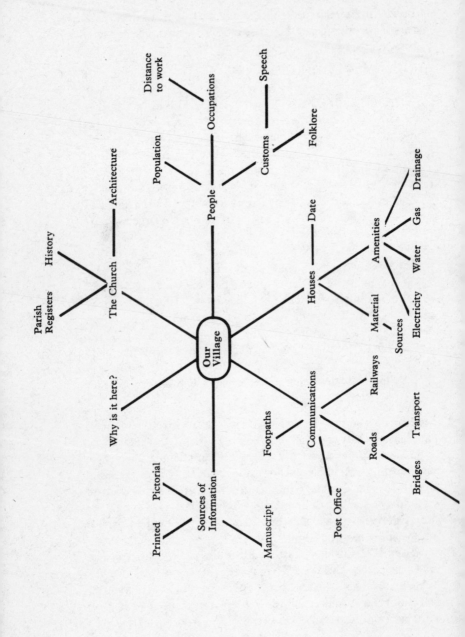

Books In countries where books are plentiful they are an essential part of a good project. They enable the children to check their own first-hand information and to amplify it, to make acquaintance with expertise, to break into and to respect and enjoy the world of learning. If they are to achieve this result, the books must be of the best possible kind, accurate and scholarly at whatever level they are directed; they must be numerous enough to allow real consultation or the children will simply copy out passages from them into their notebooks; and they must be freely available. They need not necessarily be 'school' books. School C, described in Chapter 5, used almost exclusively standard works borrowed from the County library and, in theory, much too difficult for the children. The motivation provided by the project was strong enough to make them ready to tackle a language and style which were 'grown-up'. In many ways this kind of borrowing is to be preferred to the purchase of books for the school. A proper supply of books is expensive and, if everything has to be bought, there may be a severe limitation on choice of subject matter and a strong temptation to repeat the same project year after year.

In countries where books are few and where the oral tradition and oral transmission of custom and history are predominant, it is clear that the latter must be used. This is a limitation in that it confines the project to the local or tribal sphere. Nevertheless, it is better that children should begin by using the elements of their own culture and thus come to understand and appreciate it, rather than those of an alien culture, accessible to them only through such pictorial material as can be obtained and the generally second-hand knowledge of their teachers.

A third case exists in some of the developing countries where the social structure is such that the family or tribal system has broken up and, with it, the oral culture. The latter has not yet been replaced by a book, or highly developed literary, culture. Such a society is partially cut off both from its own roots and from the fruits of other cultures. This is a very dangerous situation for any society to be in, and it is not confined to developing countries but may be found in patches, sometimes large and numerous, elsewhere. A hint as to how it may be dealt with in the primary schools may be discovered in The Liverpool (England) E.P.A.

project[14] where, in a community having some of the characteristics indicated, the children and their parents have found, in the study of their immediate neighbourhood and its problems, an interest and a social consciousness that had hitherto been lacking. Books, in such a situation, are needed and indeed come to be demanded, but a beginning can be made with a few or none if the teacher is able and permitted to show initiative.

Writing The experience and knowledge gained both at first-hand in the field and from books must be written up by each individual child. With very young children this writing up may consist mainly of the collection, in a notebook, of illustrative material, including cuttings from newspapers and magazines—but at every stage their notebooks should contain some original writing. This may, for young children, be no more than a sentence or two about a picture or a list of things seen, but the notebook will be a personal production, not a series of dictated or copied or mimeographed notes. As the children grow older, more will be written and the book may well run to many pages and form, for the time being, the principal writing activity of the group. A project should be a serious piece of work and treated as such; without plenty of writing it can hardly be so.

Exhibition A project should not fizzle out, as far too many do. It should be brought to some kind of climax, however simple. An exhibition of the work done, accompanied by a group discussion, which would include questions such as 'What have we learned from what we have done?', 'What have we left out?', 'What shall we do next?', is one way of achieving this. Another would be the production of a book, for which the individual books would be a preparation. A school in a small market town in England wrote a splendid history of their town in an enormous book which they bound and illustrated themselves. This represented a year's work and became a treasured possession of the school library.

Children like to feel that their work is important and appreciated. If all of it is done in exercise books, marked with red ink and then thrown away at the end of term, they may well accept the implied valuation of it as something ephemeral and unimportant. Children whose work is put into the school library will not only feel appreciated but will have learned that work must be well done and that it is worth doing well. In such circumstances a teacher who knows how to make the most of the opportunities will be able to demand and obtain far higher standards of presentation than one who regards the ruled exercise book as the best place for children to write in.

It will be apparent that a project which satisfies these six conditions does not fit very easily into a set time-table, which would inevitably interrupt the work and prevent the sustained concentration which it needs. In schools where the free day is well established this presents no difficulties but to a teacher who is taking the first steps from formality to freedom the prospect may look a little daunting. Many years ago a device was suggested by the late Nancy Catty, a teacher at Goldsmith's College, London, which many found useful at this early stage.[15] This was to divide the time-table into 'teacher's time' and 'children's time'. In the former the teacher could be as formal and traditional as he liked. In the latter the children had some choice both as to what they did and how they did it and how they disposed of the time. Obviously, this device allows for a wide disparity of practice. The proportions as between the two 'times' can vary enormously and the amount of genuine free choice in 'children's time' may be great or little.

What in fact happened was that either the teacher abandoned it almost at once, being unable to understand or work it, or that the barrier between the two 'times' began to break down. The children needed more time for their activities and more help from the teacher. The teacher began to see how what he did in his time could contribute to, and be given purpose by, what the children did in theirs. He discovered that the children had a capacity for working on their own and how important was discussion both with him and among themselves. Before very long the 'times' were almost indistinguishable from each other.

The device had been a useful model for a change, but it was self-destroying and paved the way for a less artificial way of teaching and learning. Those who are still in the formal stage may find it a useful framework for innovation.

Chapter 8
Reading

Although the foregoing chapters deal, by implication if not directly, with the 3 Rs, they do not cover the acquisition of reading, writing and mathematical skills. Children must learn to read, to write and to calculate. These have been the basic, sometimes the only, concerns of primary schools in all countries and, whatever changes are made in curriculum and method, they remain essential needs. Many books have been written on all three skills and it is neither desirable nor possible to deal thoroughly with them here. I propose to indicate the kind of change which has taken place in English primary schools in the initial teaching of the 3 Rs during the past half-century and what problems have had to be solved and to show how these fit in with the general approach so far described. This can be no more than an introduction to a long and complicated story, but it seems necessary to include it because it is precisely fears about what will happen to the 3 Rs which beset those who are standing on the brink of innovation.

In the course of history the great majority of people who have tried to learn to read systematically have succeeded, whatever method of teaching them has been used. Illiteracy has, in the main, been a product of no schooling rather than of inefficient teaching or method. The alphabetic method of teaching reading in English-speaking countries, that is, the method of spelling out words using the *names* of characters (ay, bee, see, dee, ee, eff) would now be universally rejected, yet it was used for centuries with successful results. New methods have been, and are being, introduced and for each strong claims have been made. Most of those who have been subjected to these methods in all their variety have learned to read. It appears, then, that for the majority (estimates might vary from seventy to ninety per cent) method is of minor importance. It does appear, however, that it increases in importance as we move down the scale of intelligence, cultural endowment, parental interest and the like and that failure to learn to read, that is, failure to respond to systematic attempts to teach reading, in the deprived minority may be caused, partially at least, by the use of inefficient methods. To make a precise estimate of the causes of failure in every individual case is difficult, perhaps impossible, but classroom practice, methods used and, of course, the particular reading book selected are all important and need careful thought by the teacher.

The first change that has taken place in England (to which it is not confined) in the past fifty years has been a recognition of the importance of what is often called the pre-reading period, the weeks or months which precede the first systematic attempt to teach reading. It was not uncommon fifty years ago, and in some countries it is the practice still, for children to arrive at school on the first day of their first term and to be given a reading lesson. They might never have looked at a book before, some might have come from homes in which there were no books and in which no one ever read a book or, in some countries, where no one was able to read. Yet, at the age of five or six, they were expected to know what a book was for and to be motivated to tackle the complex process of reading it.

The conviction that it is important and useful to know how to read was firmly implanted, even in children who had seen little evidence to support it, and large numbers survived the drudgery and boredom of the early stages and became literate, in the sense that they could read a popular newspaper. Yet only for a minority did reading become a pleasure and a means of exploring and sharing in human knowledge and art. The problem was thus twofold: how to reduce to a minimum the proportion of children who left the primary school with reading difficulties and how to increase to the maximum the number of those who, having learned to read, used their ability with profit and pleasure. The solution of the former was clearly a prerequisite of solving the latter.

The account that follows is in a logical but not a chronological order. The process of change was one of trial and error and did not follow a previously thought-out programme. In retrospect it can be seen as a series of logical steps; and to describe it thus is the simplest way to help those who wish to understand it.

The pre-reading period is seen as one in which the children become acquainted with books, find some interest in them and begin to ask questions about the meanings of printed words. The first requirement is books, mainly of pictures but with printed captions. The pictures will be illustrative, many of them photographs, and the aim will be to provide only material of really good quality. The books will be available to the children to look at, to handle, to ask questions about, to use. To begin with, no attempt is made by the teacher to teach; but when a child asks, 'What does that say?' he will be told and will be encouraged to ask it again. The frequency of such questions and the extent to which words once seen are recognised when seen again will inform the teacher of the moment when a particular child is ready for something more systematic.

Varied attempts have been made to lay down, if not rules, at any rate firmly defined guide-lines as to the stage or age at which children should learn to read. At one time it was widely believed that it should be postponed until the seventh year or to the mental age of six. At the other extreme has been a more recent theory that children can be taught to read at a very early age, three or even two, and that this should actually be done. It is, however, generally accepted that reading should be postponed until a fair degree of oral fluency and a vocabulary of at least two thousand words have been achieved, that to force a child into reading prematurely is a mistake and that to hold him back when he is obviously ready for it is equally mistaken. Systems which are centrally controlled and require reading to begin at a specified age or stage and to follow a prescribed course cannot make the adaptation to the needs of the individual child which is possible in systems which allow the teacher to use his own judgement.

The early reading primers were based on the belief that short words are easier to read than long ones. They contained such sentences as 'The man in the dell has a bell to sell: go Nell and buy the bell from the man in the dell' and 'The big ox is in a bog.

A fly is on the ox.' We now know that short words in such heavy concentrations are difficult for children. They look very alike (dell, bell; big, bog; in, is; ox, on); they form artificial and unrhythmical English sentences; and a large number of them are operators with no easily definable meanings. Further, no literate adult reads words by following the succession of characters. He recognises the whole word, unless it is quite unfamiliar, and he takes in groups of words simultaneously or nearly simultaneously. It was found that children could do the same thing and this led to the adoption of a method of reading known as 'look-and-say' with a later development called 'the sentence method'.

Briefly, the 'look-and-say' method works as follows. As soon as children begin asking, 'What does that word say?', single words, and, later, phrases and sentences are presented to them; first perhaps as labels on various objects in the classroom, e.g. door, cupboard, window, this is the door, the books are in the cupboard, the window is made of glass, or as news, e.g. it is raining today, George has a new little sister, the hyacinth bulbs are showing up; then, in response to individual requests, e.g. How, do you write . . . ?' 'Show me how you write'. The words and phrases will be those that the children need and will thus always be closely associated with their referents. They will be recognised but not spelt out.

It has been claimed that the continuation and expansion of these bodies of needed, recognised, unanalysed words will in due course teach children to read independently. While it is true that some intelligent children, placed in very fortunate circumstances, do learn to read without further systematic teaching, it has not been found that the majority can do so, because the method provides no means of tackling an unfamiliar word, unfamiliar, that is, in *appearance*, one that has not previously had to be *read*. To do this an analytical process is required. The old alphabetic method, referred to above, was analytic. Suppose the unfamiliar word was 'fireplace'. This would be spelt out eff, eye, are, ee, pee, ell, ay, see, ee—sounds which, of course, bear little resemblance to those of the word. It was this fact which led to an attempt to make the names of the characters approximate to their sounds, as has always been done in European countries. So the children were taught to say fer, eye, rer, er, per, ler, ah, ser, er, or rather that is what they *did* say, because all attempts failed to reduce to a vestige the vowel sounds unavoidably involved in vocalising the names of the consonants. The result was perhaps a little nearer to the sound of the word, though not much, and children did and still do learn to arrive at a correct or moderately correct sounding of words by the use of this analytical or phonic method. For many years, before the introduction* of 'look-and-say', all reading was learned phonically, but the phonic method, used to the exclusion of all others, has some inherent disadvantages, besides an additional one peculiar to, or specially acute in, the reading of English, which will be mentioned later.

First of all, to split up the sounds of a word in such a way that each *letter* is given equal value is a clumsy, indeed a barbarous, proceeding which can only be excused if it is a means to an end which is discarded at the earliest possible moment. Secondly, an exclusively phonic approach tends to breed an unrhythmical, staccato style of reading which may persist into adult life. The eye moves steadily from word to word or from syllable to syllable with such a concentration on vocalisation that children who have read a page in this fashion are often quite unable to recall any of the content of what they have read.

The method in most general use in English infant schools today is to begin with 'look-and-say' until a reading vocabulary of about two hundred words is acquired and children are able to read short phrases and sentences in a rhythmical, fluent manner; and then give them as much phonic teaching as they need in order to read independently. This systematic *teaching* is given in a context of plentiful reading matter. In addition to the course books, that is, books designed expressly for systematic teaching, there will be a great number of books available to the children at all times, of stories and of information and with vocabularies and sentence-forms suited to the stages they have reached. Without this library of books the systematic teaching will be hindered by the lack of opportunity of profiting from it. Some teachers manage without course books altogether and use the library books for their systematic teaching, but the majority prefer

* It was invented in the seventeenth century.

to have a series of graded readers (i.e. a course) as some kind of assurance of systematic progress.

We must now return to the disadvantage of the phonic method peculiar to, or specially acute in, reading English. English is the L1 (or mother tongue) of the inhabitants of a considerable portion of the globe, as well as being the lingua franca of countries in Asia and Africa where a multiplicity of native languages makes a lingua franca indispensable. Any difficulty in reading English has an importance therefore that extends far beyond the United Kingdom or even the English-speaking (L1) peoples.

For historical reasons the spelling of English is highly idiosyncratic and a prime source of irritation to non-English students. A language in which the words *thought, rough, drought, cough, though, thorough* and *through* all have different vowel sounds corresponding to the combination *ough* is open to the charge of almost wilful perversity. It must be said that inconsistency of sign and sound is not confined to English, but it *is* more characteristic of English than of other European languages. The need for an alphabet which would make it possible to write any language phonetically has long been recognised. The international phonetic alphabet and one or two other such alphabets are in general use by linguists; but, although theoretically they might replace the Roman alphabet, which, with a few local variants, is used in most parts of the world outside Greece, Russia, China, Japan and the Arabic-speaking countries, the practical difficulties of making such a vast change have always seemed insurmountable. The same objection applies to the many ingenious alphabets invented from time to time since the late sixteenth century and to the alternative of a reformed spelling which retains the Roman alphabet. President Theodore Roosevelt's well-meaning but misguided efforts towards very moderate reform in 1906 have done no good to anyone and irreparable damage to the interchangeability of English and American editions.

One attempt to create a logical alphabet stands out from all the rest and demands more detailed treatment. This is the Initial Teaching Alphabet (i.t.a.) of Sir James Pitman. This differs from all others in that it eliminates all upper case characters (capitals are replaced by enlarged lower case characters), in that it uses forty-four characters of which twenty-six are the familiar Roman letters and the remainder are either digraphs or very simple, almost self-evident modifications of Roman letters and, finally, in that it is *not* designed as a reformed alphabet for universal adoption but solely as an aid to learning which is discarded when reading has been learned. It is no more difficult for children to learn than the Roman alphabet and an adult familiar with the latter can read it almost at sight and can learn to write it in an hour or two. The first half of this assertion may be tested at once by the following passage:

ʃhe iniʃhial teeᴄhiŋ alfabet has been desiend wiʃh ʃhe siŋgl purpos ov simplifieiŋ ʃhe task ov lerniŋ tꙮ reed iŋgliʃh. as sꙮn as flꙮensy in reediŋ with ʃhe nue alfabet has been acheevd, a transiʃhon is mæd tꙮ reediŋ wiʃh ʃhe orʇhodoks rœman alfabet(s). i.t.a. dus not pretend tꙮ bee a nue meʇhod ov teeᴄhiŋ; it is meerly a nue meedium ʃhat can mæk aull ʃhe egsistiŋ meʇhods ov teeᴄhiŋ mor effectiv.

When it was proposed that the alphabet should be tried out in English infant schools, every conceivable objection was raised. It was said that children would find the characters difficult to learn, that they would encounter great difficulty in transferring to traditional orthography (t.o.) once having learned i.t.a., that their spelling would suffer, that they learned to read satisfactorily anyhow so that there was no need for this kind of help and that, since they were surrounded by notices, advertisements, newspapers and other matter all in t.o. they would be hopelessly confused by i.t.a. All these objections proved to be groundless. The pioneer experiments all showed that children learned to read more quickly in i.t.a., that failure to learn was almost eliminated and that no subsequent disadvantages revealed themselves. An exhaustive enquiry by two independent researchers came to the conclusion that, for the great majority of children, better results, even much better results, flowed from using i.t.a. than from using t.o. as a learning medium.[16] It is probably true to say that no teaching device has ever been subjected to such a rigorous scrutiny as i.t.a. and that, though other and better ways of learning to read may be discovered, i.t.a. is for the majority of children the best now available.[17]

The importance of i.t.a. for those who are learning to read English as a second language (L2) is self-evident. Each character represents an unvarying sound, so that the seven words containing the combination *ough* mentioned above now look like this:

ꜧhaut	(thought)
ruf	(rough)
drout	(drought)
kof	(cough)
ꜱhœ	(though)
ꜧhuru	(thorough)
ꜧhrω	(through)

It will be noticed that the alphabet distinguishes between the unvoiced (ꜧh) and the voiced (ꜱh) and that the silent *gh* in *thought, drought, though, thorough* and *through* is eliminated. The Scottish *loch* and the Irish *lough* which both mean *lake* and are both pronounced with a velar fricative consonant not found in standard English (cf. *bach* in German and the very similar *Juan* in Spanish) would both be written lok in i.t.a. which, for simplicity's sake, does not include characters for regional and slight variations.

The i.t.a. has now been adopted by about fifteen per cent of English infant schools and its use is spreading in the United States of America, South Africa and elsewhere. Of schools which have adopted it only a tiny percentage have abandoned it and then for administrative and not educational reasons. It is not supposed that this fact or the foregoing brief account will convince the reader and lead to his adopting i.t.a. My purpose has been simply to say enough to persuade him to look further into the matter for himself, to examine both the alphabet and the evidence and to draw his own conclusions.

The changes described earlier involve the supply of certain materials before they can be effected:

Teacher-made materials The words, phrases and sentences used in the first 'look-and-say' stage are best made by individual teachers to suit the needs of their children. Urban and rural children need different words. Classrooms contain different objects. Children's interests vary. A set of words, phrases and sentences produced by an education department or a publisher would therefore be of much more limited value than a home-made collection.

Library books It has been shown in Chapter 7 how essential is a good supply of books to the kind of general approach here recommended. It must be emphasised that this is true of every stage of education, including the pre-reading stage. The books may not be kept in a library and for younger children will certainly not be, but they must be thought of as books in a library are thought of, as being there and readily available to serve every need and interest which children are likely to have, the unusual as well as the usual.

Course books The books used for the systematic teaching of reading must be adapted to the methods employed. It is not advisable to change over to a mixed 'look-and-say' followed by phonic method and retain phonic readers planned as primers. To choose between the numerous different courses is not easy. A good many of them are satisfactory in a formal way; that is, the vocabulary is well graded and the repetition of words well controlled. The illustrations in some are very inferior; and, considered as examples of English and as providing the beginnings of literary experience, many are found wanting. Rather than offer specific advice which would inevitably be out of date before this book was published I prefer to advise the careful scrutiny of a large number of courses, taking into account format, print, illustration and durability as well as the literary facilities and content and the seeking of advice, if possible, from practising teachers with experience of using the courses.

i.t.a. If i.t.a. is to be used, it will be necessary to have not only course books printed in i.t.a. but also library material. This is readily available but considerable financial outlay is involved and, if i.t.a. is introduced, it must not fail from shortage of material.

In the setting of the progressive primary school, teachers have been able, indeed obliged, to look at reading in a wider way and on a longer-term basis. They have had to give up seeing it solely as a skill to be taught and mastered and to realise that, from the very beginning, it ought to be a pleasure and must be taught in such a way as to lead on to the kind of reading which is not only an essential part of all education, but which can be, for some if not for all, a part of life. This wider and longer view has sometimes been taken at the expense of systematic teaching of the skill, a mistake for which the children pay dearly, but not one that it is difficult to avoid or is inherent in the approach.

Chapter 9
Writing

Although it is much more important for the majority of people to be able to speak well and read easily than to write, writing is an essential part of education and one in which teachers are very sensitive about results. Written work can be kept for comparison, taken away, scrutinised by other teachers, parents and inspectors, and judged by clearly defined standards of calligraphy and grammar and by rather vaguer, though often strongly held, beliefs about literary style.

For many years the teaching of writing in England was based on a theory which, though apparently logical, took little account of the way in which children learn. It was held that both calligraphy and composition were difficult and that the process of learning them must be slow. The muscular control of the small movements required to form written characters fluently and in the accepted style was found to be lacking in young children and acquired slowly. The solution was thought to be copy-writing. I can remember having to copy out eight times on double lines, in a cursive style, and using a sharp, flexible nib which had to be constantly dipped in an ink-pot, the line: 'Knowing I loved my books he furnished me.' This was not a very inspiring occupation, nor did it achieve the expected results, either in my own case or in that of many of my contemporaries. Our handwriting was mostly abominable and some of it still is.

In many schools, pencils were used during the first two or three years and, when pens were introduced, they had all to be of the same kind. The holders were too small in diameter to be gripped comfortably and the nibs were spiky and soft. Fountain pens were forbidden. There was also a widespread uniformity of style, the most popular being what was known as the Civil Service hand. This consisted of characters which were all joined in every word (any gap, however natural, was condemned). The characters *b*, *f*, *g*, *h*, *k*, *l*, *y* and sometimes *z* all had to have loops which gave a top or bottom-heavy look to them since, for some unfathomable reason, the length of the loops had to be twice the height of the body of the letter. Furthermore, all downstrokes had to be thick and upstrokes thin, an effect produced by pressure on the nib. This hand, at its best, had a certain mechanical elegance but it was rarely seen at its best. It was almost impossible to write it quickly and, as soon as it was used for anything but a calligraphic exercise, it tended to deteriorate into an untidy scrawl. This led to the bad habit of fair copies. The children wrote their compositions in 'rough' books which were often dirty, ill-kept and almost illegible and then copied them into the exercise books which were shown to visitors, a deadening process which reduced the amount of free composition by half.

By 1930 the majority of infant schools had abandoned the practice just described and had introduced what was called script writing. This introduction was primarily made in the interests of reading, not of calligraphy. There are small differences between the written and printed forms of characters in English. They are much less marked than in German and Russian but they were believed to constitute an obstacle to reading. Script writing used most of the printed forms and had no ligatures between the letters. The size of the letters was gradually reduced as the children advanced. The resultant hand was quite pleasant in appearance but unsuitable for speed. When the children left the infant school it was abandoned and they had to learn the cursive Civil Service hand.

The developments in composition to be described later brought matters to a crisis. Neither of the hands traditionally taught was suitable if children were going to write at a reasonable speed and in the quantity expected and, at the same time, with a progressively elegant calligraphy. A fair number of individual schools have found a satisfactory solution but it cannot be claimed that many have. The almost universal use of the ball-point pen, with which it is difficult, though not impossible, to write a good hand, has introduced a new setback. In the matter of calligraphy the freedom of the individual teacher operates disadvantageously. It is one in which a basic uniformity is needed to ensure that children are not obliged by the whim of the teacher to change the style they have originally been taught.

I am now going to describe what seems to be, in broad terms, the best solution, as I have seen it in individual schools and groups of schools. The style of handwriting to be adopted must be one of which the basic letter forms taught from the beginning do not change radically as they come to be used by adults. A partial exception must be made for i.t.a. which involves the shedding of a few characters in the later stages and the learning of the t.o. capitals, neither of which seems to cause the children any trouble. The basis in any case is the Roman letter. The style is one of the group of formal hands, originating in the sixteenth century, known as Italic. This style requires the use of a chisel-ended nib, either square or obliquely cut, which makes the thickness of a stroke depend upon the direction in which the pen is moving and not on the varying pressure which is so tiring to the hand muscles. The style must be learned and used by all the teachers and all the children, though a child coming from another school who could write well in a different style would obviously not be forced to adopt the new one.

In the early stages the children form the letters separately without ligatures, using a soft pencil or even charcoal. A model alphabet is permanently displayed in the classroom and the children use this and imitate the teacher. Practice is provided by composition rather than by calligraphic exercises and when improvement is not automatic it is achieved by careful correction. All writing is on plain, unlined paper and the virtues of level lines, spacing, margination and approximate regularity of size are acquired by practice. One of the errors perpetuated by writing on ruled lines is the belief that absolute regularity is a virtue. It is in printing. It is not in calligraphy, as may be seen by studying any good piece of adult handwriting.

The joining of letters develops automatically with speed. Here again the teacher provides a model but does not insist on any unbreakable rule. There is room for some individuality here, always provided that clarity and elegance are preserved.

The result that may be confidently expected from this kind of approach is a high average standard of calligraphy in the school and a very low failure rate. It will be necessary to tolerate, in the early stages, handwriting which does not conform to all the virtues expected later, but at every stage improvement can be and ought to be looked for and a bad writer among the ten-year-olds should be an exception. Handwriting is a craft. The beautiful brush calligraphy of China and Japan, where it is looked upon as an art, is a reminder of this which the utilitarian West badly needs. It is possible to imagine an era when everybody uses a typewriter and children are taught typing and not handwriting. Calligraphy would then become a luxury or hobby like fencing or painting. Few countries have yet reached a stage when such a development looks near. In the meantime children need to be taught to write quickly, clearly and (I hope we can agree on this) elegantly. The day-to-day practice can be varied by undertakings which require a specially good calligraphic standard, the writing of invitations, of programmes and menus for Open Days, the copying of some treasured poem or prose passage. These, it is true, are in a sense exercises, but they have a purpose which makes good handwriting more than just an aim in itself, and they need not have the repetitive characteristic that was such a boring, and indeed harmful, feature of the old copy-books.

The traditional methods of teaching calligraphy and composition involved very slow progress towards the aims of neatness, clarity, elegance, correct syntax, spelling, style and fluency. In some schools *all* the written work up to the age of eight consisted of exercises, dictation, reproduction and spelling, and included no writing in which the children were using their own language to record what they had done or seen, to express what they felt, to make poems or stories or to communicate with other people apart from their teacher. For three years they were preparing for something of which they had no experience or evidence that it would be enjoyable when it was once learned; this, despite the facts that they could mostly read with some ease by the time they were seven and could nearly all speak with fluency and a considerable command of language.

At the time of which I am writing, 'free' composition, when it made its appearance in the eight-year-old classes, consisted of short passages on themes chosen by the teacher. These were on such topics as: What I do on Saturdays, What I did in the holidays, Dressing a doll, My pet, How I help mother, A rainy day, and Spring. The emphasis was still on the formal elements and only exceptionally gifted children were able to overcome the obstacles to good composition which this emphasis and these well-worn topics presented. Attempts were sometimes made to elicit imaginative writing by setting topics like My most exciting adventure, Ghost stories and Sunsets, but such invitations were equally ineffective except with the children who did not need them.

The changes in the teaching of composition which have taken place in a large number of English primary schools in the last quarter of a century have been indicated at various points in earlier chapters. It may be useful to summarise them and to discuss some of the problems with which the innovators had to contend.

The first and most important change was an enormous increase in the writing output of children at every stage. Whereas ten-year-olds in the '30s would perhaps fill one or at most two exercise books a year (and this represented their total output), children of the same age nowadays write many hundreds of pages. The justification for this increased bulk was, at first, a guess that, if children learned to speak primarily by speaking, as was self-evident, the same might be true of writing; that, unless they wrote a great deal, they would have insufficient practice to learn effectively. This guess turned out to be well-founded. Children astonished their teachers by the amount they wrote if given the chance and by the interesting content of their writing. What worried the innovators and drove the traditionalists to scornful disbelief was the effect on the formal elements. It had at one time been the habit of inspectors to look at these very critically and, in particular, to comment adversely on any failure on the teacher's part to correct faults, whether of spelling or grammar; and, although this habit had been for many years modified and even abandoned, it still produced a phobia in the teachers' minds.

We have seen that, so far as calligraphy was concerned, a lower standard of letter-formation, regularity and spacing had to be accepted in the early stages in return for fluency and quantity and that this need not lead to a permanent lowering but rather to something ultimately much better than had been accepted in the past. This was not an automatic result. It needed careful planning and good teaching. If we look at the other formal elements, spelling, punctuation and grammar, we find the same to be broadly true.

Spelling has always loomed very large in the consciousness of English teachers. The particular difficulties of English spelling already discussed are no doubt responsible for this. It may be useful to mention the effect upon spelling of learning to read and write in i.t.a. To quote from Warburton and Southgate:

> Regarding spelling in i.t.a. there is no doubt whatsoever that children found this much simpler than spelling in t.o. and that the favourable effect of this on children's written work was enormous.
>
> As far as the transfer to t.o. spelling was concerned, there was a growing belief, which was finding its way into practice, that specific, carefully-graded and quite formal teaching of t.o. spelling rules was found helpful and indeed interesting by the children. The interviewer's impressions were that, the longer the teachers' experience with i.t.a., the more likely they were to consider such spelling teaching to be necessary and the stronger were their beliefs that children's experiences with i.t.a. had conditioned them towards an appreciation of t.o. spelling rules.
>
> . . . not one infant teacher with experience of children transferring to t.o. spelling expressed the view that i.t.a. had a deleterious effect on children's spelling in t.o. . . . No evidence of a decline in spelling ability was noted in infant classes and there were certain indications of improvements.[18]

These conclusions are specially interesting since fears about spelling were one of the most persistent objections to i.t.a. raised by teachers. Indeed, Sir James Pitman himself expected that there would be a deterioration, though he considered this a price worth paying for the gains in reading.[19]

The facts about spelling, at least so far as English is concerned, seem to be these. No one is a perfect speller. Even the most practised writers occasionally make mistakes. The great majority of people who write regularly are good spellers, though they may have a number of words that they habitually spell wrongly or have to look up. A very small number of people who write regularly remain bad spellers throughout their lives. Habitual and general bad spelling is characteristic of those who write very seldom. Children thus vary between those who learn to spell with little or no formal teaching and those who resist all efforts to teach them. The conclusion seems to be that, though spelling should not become a fetish, it does need to be systematically taught to the majority and that children who have learned i.t.a. may be at a considerable advantage.[20]

Punctuation is a convention which has to be learned, though many quite literate people learn it imperfectly and are capable of stringing together main clauses joined by commas. Traditionally it was taught by exercises. Unpunctuated passages were given to the children and they were required to punctuate them. I am unaware of any research or systematic enquiry into this matter. Present practice seems to reduce instruction to a minimum and leave much to be picked up from the example of what is read and from the experience of writing. As in other skills this works with the more able children, but my impression is that more definite instruction, which need not take up much time, is needed.

It would be unwise to insist upon a high standard at too early a stage, when the conventions of writing can mean very little. The period or full-stop is clearly the first to be learned, with the comma following as sentences become lengthier. Inverted commas (quotes) are very easily learned and are too convenient to be ignored. Many people never use, or even learn the use of, the semi-colon. Eric Partridge calls it the next most useful after 'the unavoidable period and the almost indispensable comma'.[21] 'The semi-colon,' he says, 'separates one part of a sentence from the next more decisively and distinctively than does a comma; it does not however conclude a statement nor end a thought.' Such language is not likely to have much meaning for a young child and perhaps until it does it is best to leave the semi-colon alone; except perhaps for pointing out its use in examples that crop up in books. The same applies to the colon, of which Partridge writes: 'It is a rich and subtle stop, to be used with care and economy: and it rewards both writer and reader.' Most teachers would feel that, if children of, say, ten years of age use the period, the comma and the inverted commas correctly that is as much as it is reasonable to expect.

Grammar, in the sense of accidence and syntax, has for long been an educational battleground. The unquestioned necessity of teaching grammar to those who were learning a Classical (dead) language and the need for a good deal of direct teaching of grammar to those learning a foreign tongue were taken as reasons for teaching English grammar to English-speaking children, despite the facts that most of them could speak the language adequately by the time they reached school and that the grammar taught was much more relevant to Latin than to English. The reaction in the '30s led to no grammar being taught at all, an omission which often caused distress and annoyance to those teachers in secondary schools who were responsible for teaching foreign languages and who expected, or at least wished, that the children would come to them knowing the meaning of the parts of speech and the parts of a sentence (e.g. subject, object, predicate, main clause, dependent clause).

While this quite pointless argument was going on, grammar itself was undergoing a drastic re-examination by academic linguists. Not only the terminology but the whole concept of the functions of words and sentence structure was being revised: often one revision would be rejected for another. Linguistics made, and still has made, very little impact on primary teaching; but it has thrown the whole study of language into a fluid state.

Meanwhile the primary schools of England have gone on their way teaching no grammar, or very little, but getting an enormous amount of written work from the children. If this written work is examined it is found that syntactical faults are surprisingly scarce.

Consider the following piece of writing by a six-year-old girl, printed exactly as it was written:

My Wobbly Tooth

Mrs Salter [teacher] said 'Pull it out' and then she went home Then I twisted it round I twisted it agran [again] and it came out. Then I went to bed I put the tooth in the window sill. In the morning there was sixpence in the window sill it spit [? split] my gum. it Felt very soft it was so wobbly it did not bleed Mumy said that it is nearly filled up.

It will be noticed that there are only three spelling mistakes (agran, spit and Mumy) and that the punctuation, where it exists, is correct. Apart from the tense sequence in the final sentence the syntax is faultless yet it is quite inconceivable that this child could have been *taught* grammar.

We may now compare this piece of seventy-one words with the following by a seven-year-old boy:

I won a cup. It shone all year

One day I was walking down the raod and I was walking in the snow I saw a car it was going very fast and just a little way up when I saw it it was crashed up to bits the man was hurt a bit it crashed For the raod was dangerous and it made me want a car to go in snow and I bort a new car to go in snow I played with it all day then the next day there is a race for cars that go in snow and I went to it I went so fast that I won it I won it I won a cup we went home I put it on the mantlpeas it shone like gold it shone all year.

The mixture of fact and fantasy and the way in which the latter takes over and becomes ecstatic is something that we may enjoy in this little piece, and something, be it noted, which would have been improbable if not impossible in the traditional set composition. Punctuation is non-existent. There are three spelling mistakes (*raod* which occurs twice and *bort* and *mantlpeas* which are phonetically accurate). Syntactically it is faultless except for a present tense where the past is required. It contains eighteen main clauses, two with infinitive verbs depending on them and four dependent clauses with finite verbs. This is not a very developed syntactical structure but it is adequate to what the writer had to say. Once again, no formal grammar could possibly have been taught to him.

The theory upon which this way of approaching written work is based is that, provided the children have plenty of practice, provided that through reading and a variety of interests and activities they have plenty to write about, and provided that oral discussion keeps pace with composition, vocabulary and syntax will develop automatically; that is, that children will need more words and more structures and that the need will ensure the learning. There can be no doubt that, to a large extent, experience bears this out. Innumerable anthologies of children's prose and poetry are available and, if these are compared with what were regarded as good compositions thirty years ago, it will be evident that a great improvement in fluency, interest and expressiveness has taken place. It is important, however, not to allow our admiration of this improvement to blind us, not so much to shortcomings, as to the possibilities of further improvement, especially among the less gifted children whose products do not often get into the anthologies.

The Schools Council is sponsoring a project in linguistics and English teaching which has already produced some interesting material on the theory and practice of teaching initial reading and writing in which the two skills are very closely linked.[22] It would be impossible to summarise this material within the compass of this book and it is, in any case, too soon to evaluate it. The title *Breakthrough to Literacy* suggests perhaps a rather inflated claim in view of the great advances in reading and writing made since the war, but the material looks as if it has considerable possibilities and, when the whole project is complete, it will merit the serious attention of all teachers of young children.

The second great change that has come over written work in the English primary school is in the width and variety of the subject matter. This has been indicated in earlier chapters and needs no further discussion, but it may be useful to underline the problems which are bound to confront teachers who wish to follow suit. I hope that what I have written earlier will make it clear that it is not simply a question of setting subjects for composition drawn from science, mathematics, history, geography and so on. The subject matter must have been part of the children's intellectual and/or emotional experience before they can use it to write well. Confronted with a demand to discuss Henry VIII's policy in relation to the Church or the causes of the Civil War, countless secondary school children have, in the past, written a great deal of nonsense and written it very badly. Variety of subject matter is no guarantee of excellence. The general approach recommended in this book, which aims at capturing the interest and co-operation of children, at stimulating their desire to learn while leaving something to their initiative and choice, involves the use of language, oral and written, in a wide variety of forms: discussion, narrative, descriptive, reporting, imaginative, not as an exercise but as a necessity.

This may be illustrated by an example. Some eight-year-old children brought to school a dead mouse and a dead sparrow. This in itself is important since, in the traditional school, they would not have been allowed to do so or, if they had, would have been told to throw the bodies away or, at best, bury them. In this instance the interest or curiosity or whatever it was that prompted the action was used, first of all by the children's talking to the teacher about them and then by writing.

Our Sparrow

One day I was playing with our Kitten when he sprang
up because he saw a little sparrow the baby sparrow
went in the hedge and our kitten ran fast and he got the
sparrow and ran away with it. I saw him and I got
hold of the sparrow but it was too late he was dead we
put him in a box with some tissue in.

This is straightforward reporting, well expressed apart from the faulty punctuation. It may be compared with the following:

The Mouse

A Mouse is quiet and is dead and now he cannot run.
He will be dead for ever. It makes you feel sick.

In this something of the child's feelings is communicated to us. It is more than just reporting.

A third example is descriptive but also communicates feeling, though in a quite different way.

Mouse

Today Melvyn brought a mouse to school. It was
dead. He showed it to us. Its eyes were open. It was
still and quiet. It was cold. It was frozen and bony and
stiff.

Here the punctuation emphasises the simultaneous pity and

repulsion felt as each feature of the little body was observed.

The other children wrote similarly with reporting, descriptive and emotional elements in varying proportions. This was a better foundation for composition than the long course of instruction in the formal elements which was the rule thirty years ago.

All that has been written so far about composition has referred to the situation of English being taught as L1. When English is taught as L2 either in a country where it is the lingua franca, e.g. Nigeria, or in one in which it is simply a foreign language which some or most children learn, e.g. Denmark, the case is different. The children in such countries have little or none of the familiarity with syntax obtained orally by English-speaking (L1) children. Even if a purely oral approach is used during the first year of learning, the experience of using the language orally will be much less. It is not within the scope of this book, which is concerned with the actual changes made in Britain, to go into the problems of teaching English as L2. Literature and textbooks concerned with this abound. It may, however, be said that the earlier children *use* the L2 to communicate and express their own experience the better. To confine them, as is too often done, to translation, is to treat the language as a dead language and to postpone quite unnecessarily their use of it as a live one. In the early oral stages, and as soon as writing begins, the children should use English basically as they use their own language, to say what is in their minds. The written work must be treated as a reinforcement of oral work and a further reinforcement should be provided by pictures and by imaginary characters with whom the children can identify themselves.

Chapter 10
Language study

It was stated in the previous section that it is beyond the scope of this book to deal with the techniques of learning English as L2 but something ought to be said about the study of the language where it is the pupil's mother tongue (L1). In the writer's childhood English children were taught grammar. That is, they learned, or rather were supposed to learn, the definitions and uses of the parts of speech which led to parsing, i.e. the recognition of the parts of speech in a sentence and analysis of sentences and paragraphs into what would now be called syntactical structures. This practice was defended on two indefensible grounds, first, that it taught the children to speak and write correctly and, secondly, that it was an essential preliminary to the learning of a foreign language, whether classical or modern. The picture of English children speaking happily and fluently in the tongue that they had learned before arriving at school suddenly discovering that they could only do this 'properly' if they underwent one grammar lesson a week was so absurd that only the most diehard pedagogue could ever have believed it. As for the other argument, there are so many concepts in Latin, French and other grammars which have no relevance in English that it seems better to learn the grammar of a specific language rather than attempt the difficult, if not impossible, task of learning concepts which have little relevance in English simply because they are important in another language to be learned later on.

It may be well to illustrate this by an example. The concept of the object, a notional and somewhat woolly concept which modern linguistics does not use, is indicated in Latin by the use of the accusative or dative case. Latin can be neither written nor understood unless the reader knows the various flexions which signal those cases. The notion of the object has been transferred to English as if the syntactical structures of the two languages were the same or similar, instead of being widely different. In Latin flexions are vital, word-order insignificant, in conveying meaning. *Filius matrem amat* means 'the son loves the mother', no matter in what order the three words are placed. In English, word-order is vital and flexions very few: 'The cat chases the dog'; 'the dog chases the cat'. To define the object in English as 'the receiver of the action' or 'that which is affected by the verb', two common definitions, is inaccurate and misleading. Children are supplied with examples such as, 'I strike the table' and 'I break the stick' which are special cases in which a syntactical relationship coincides, so to speak, with a physical one. They understand the physical one and indeed can demonstrate it convincingly but, if the examples had been 'I see the moon', 'I remember 1939', 'I feel the heat,' 'I hear the bell,' they would have been hard put to it to understand, let alone explain the relationship, though the meaning presents no difficulty. To over-simplify what is, in reality, very complicated serves no good purpose. The children do not learn anything useful or important and acquire mistaken notions which may be obstacles to later study.

The question is: What attempt should be made to introduce children of primary school age to material classifiable under syntax, flexion, semantics, philology, phonetics, metaphor, as part of a systematic study? It may be argued that children of this age are not ready for this kind of study at all, that they should be concerned with using, enjoying and understanding their mother tongue without any attempt to understand how it works. This negative position is certainly to be preferred to the mechanical and inaccurate grammar lessons of the old kind, and equally to a premature excursion into the terminology and corresponding intricacies of modern linguistics. I feel very doubtful whether anything in the shape of a systematic course of language study is desirable at this stage. Such courses have a fatal tendency to be mechanical and to substitute testing for insight or, to speak metaphorically, medicine for food. What is needed is not a course or a textbook but a teacher who has some knowledge of linguistics and an interest in and sensitivity to language, who will be able to sense the endless opportunities as they arise, who is capable not just of instructing but of illuminating. A teacher who cannot do this would probably be well advised to leave language study to someone who can.[23]

Chapter 11
Mathematics

It is in mathematics teaching that the most dramatic and wide-spread changes have taken place in English primary schools since the Second World War. A combination of influences brought this about and the subject, which in 1945 was perhaps the most conservative in method and content, has become the most revolutionary. It is beyond the scope of this chapter to describe how this happened; it is with the changes themselves that we are concerned.

Traditionally, mathematics was taught in an almost purely mechanical way: tables were memorised and operations were carried out according to rules which were seldom explained. Children embarked, almost from the start, on learning the two times table up to 2×12 and then proceeded to the three times and so on. The relationship between tables, e.g. 2 and 4, 5 and 10, 3 and 6 and the relationship between 12 and 2, 3, 4 and 6 were seldom pointed out or made use of. Sums were equally mechanical and it was usual for all the four fundamental operations to be learned and practised mechanically before any of them was used for any practical purpose whatever. When they had been learned they were applied, equally mechanically, to money. The English money system made this a laborious process; and the various tables of length, volume, weight and capacity which also had to be learned involved further complication. The recent adoption of the decimal system (the duodecimal would have been far better but was clearly impracticable) has removed this difficulty. Finally, after this long course of mechanical learning and working, the children reached Problems. These were supposed to be practical but too often they were simply mechanical sums wrapped up in words,

I bought two shillings' worth of sugar, six-penny worth of biscuits, half-a-crown's worth of bacon and two 2d boxes of matches. I gave the grocer a ten-shilling note. How much change did I receive?

or concerned with situations often grotesquely unreal or irrelevant, such as filling baths with the wastepipe open or installing a telegraph wire between London and Birmingham.

Some children learned these mechanical processes with great success and produced exercise books of neatly and correctly worked sums without ever acquiring much understanding of mathematics. Some left school with little more than an ability to give and demand correct change, calculate wages and perform simple measuring and weighing operations, a body of knowledge which was perfectly adequate for most of their daily needs and could have been acquired much more quickly and with much less waste of energy. Some progressed beyond the elementary stages and learned real mathematics. Some developed a mathematical phobia which lasted all their lives so that, when asked in public to do even the simplest sum, they would be liable to falter and even be reduced to shamed silence.

I have described the system and its results in oversimplified terms. It was not always as bad as that and there were enlightened teachers who struck out on their own, but the description is basically true. The changes which have taken place in content and method have been described in detail in numbers of books and all that I propose to do is to give some indication of their nature.

Whereas the traditional approach was abstract and assumed that the basic facts of number, e.g. $2 + 1 = 3$, $3 - 1 = 2$, $3 - 2 = 1$, would be easily grasped by little children, the modern approach is concrete. The assumption that the connection between the three expressions just quoted is self-evident to little children was found to be false, and other apparently obvious mathematical facts proved to be equally difficult for children to grasp. Mechanical learning had to some extent disguised this failure to understand. The composition of the numbers 2 to 10, which had been gaily learned by rote, was now seen to need much more time and trouble. The long-established use of beads as a concrete aid to addition and subtraction gave way to a much greater variety of objects, natural and devised. The abstraction was gradually built up from the concrete. Children had to learn that two cows in one field and three in another made five cows, that if one of the cows was moved from one field to the other there were still five cows, that if two horses were put into the field containing three cows the field contained five animals, and so on. To many teachers this seemed a very slow business. It was slow but it was not tedious, because it was not given as a series of lessons in a period devoted entirely to mathematics but in all sorts of situations, play, physical education, nature study, expeditions. This does not mean that it was simply left to be picked up casually. The teachers seized opportunities but they also gave systematic instruction. Furthermore, mathematical knowledge needed practice before it could be so completely assimilated as to be taken for granted.

The classroom shop, a common feature of English infant schools, provides a useful example of how the approach works. The shop is not just a piece of mathematical apparatus. It involves, or can involve, knowledge of the goods sold, e.g. where oranges and sugar come from and the use of language, spoken and written. It may involve art and craft if it is home-made. Mathematically it provides opportunities for real measuring and weighing, for simple calculations of quantity and price, for accurate recording of stock and takings, and it has the great advantage of being adaptable to the varying capacities of the children. Classroom shops are not always very imaginatively used but their possibilities are very great and intelligent teachers know how to exploit them.

There are many other ways in which concrete mathematical experience can be gained. The concepts of likeness and difference can only be fully grasped by experiencing them in a variety of forms; and this imposes upon the teacher the task of recognising and using the possibilities inherent in day-to-day situations and of seeing that experience thus gained is fitted into a framework of systematic knowledge and consolidated by practice.

Children taught in this way make a slow start but obtain a sound basis. They often show a surprising interest in abstract mathematics; for example, in number series, and considerable perception in identifying these. By using histograms and graphs at a much earlier stage than used to be the case they learn to think in terms of curves and are much readier to tackle algebra than were children of an older generation for whom it was postponed until the age of twelve or thirteen. The ease and confidence with which they handle binary arithmetic or indeed arithmetic of any other base astonishes their elders.

It must not be supposed that these happy results are automatic. They depend not only upon the skill and perception of the teacher but also upon his mathematical knowledge. This knowledge need not be very extensive. He need not be in the full sense of the word a mathematician but he must be able to think mathematically. In England a large number of short courses in mathematics have been arranged for teachers who, though able to teach the old mechanical arithmetic, quailed before the new methods and content. The results have shown that, given such provision, a dramatic and widespread change is possible in quite a short period.

It will be asked what place there is for didactic teaching, for memorisation and for practice. This is best answered by reference to the learning of the composition of 10, which was an invariable feature of first year mathematics in English infant schools. The children could be heard chanting '9 and 1 are 10, 8 and 2 are 10, 7 and 3 are 10' and so on. They were then questioned: 'What do 7 and 3 make?' 'What must be added to 4 to make 10?' After a little more practice, oral and written, they were believed to 'know' the composition of 10. They rarely learned:

$$7 + 2 + 1 = 10$$
$$6 + 3 + 1 = 10$$
$$5 + 3 + 2 = 10$$
$$5 + 4 + 1 = 10$$

and almost never:

$$1 + 2 + 3 + 4 = 10$$

The knowledge gained, moreover, was seldom applied. Except as practice material for easy addition and subtraction, it was never used. I have frequently asked 10-year-old children and classes of adults, taught in this way, for the sum of $1 + 2 + 3 + 4 + 5 + 6 + 7 + 8 + 9 + 10$ and have found scarcely one who made use of the knowledge obtained in the infant school. Nearly all laboriously added up the ten numbers.

Nowadays, the learning of the composition of 10 would have been preceded by a great deal of what is usually called 'number experience', that is, the handling, counting and measuring of objects and materials in such a way that ideas of quantity became firmly established in the children's minds. They would have learned about all the numbers up to 10, how they were composed, what happened when you divided them up (e.g. 5 marbles cannot be made to balance scales but 5 ounces of sugar can). They would have discovered that even + even = even, odd + odd = even, odd + even = odd, and would know, by experiment, that this is invariable. They would arrange the numbers in such a way that they made 5 elevens.

1 + 10, 2 + 9, 3 + 8, 4 + 7, 5 + 6,

and 5 tens + 1 five

10, 9 + 1, 8 + 2, 7 + 3, 6 + 4; + 5

They would see, by the use of a 10 × 10 number square, that the second ten numbers (11 to 20) added up to 100 more than the first ten. (The commonest answer to a question on this is 110, clear evidence that the basic facts of number are not understood.)

They might even learn and try out the formula $S = \dfrac{n}{2} (L + 1)$,

something that in the traditional school would have had no place until a very much later stage.

It will be observed that in all this, deliberate memorisation plays a very small part and that practice, although vital, can be kept down to the limits of necessity and not be allowed to take up too much of the available time.

A similar approach is made to the learning of the multiplication table. It is clear that a time must come when all the number bonds, anyhow up to 10 × 10 or 12 × 12, are known and can be repeated without hesitation. The necessary knowledge is built up by use and familiarity and reinforced by understanding. The 10 × 10 square can be used for the formalisation of this knowledge, the tables being filled in on a blank square, thus showing the particular pattern that each one makes and the relationship between them. The stage of memorisation, when it is reached, should present very few difficulties.

Williams and Shuard, two distinguished mathematicians who have given much thought and attention to the teaching of mathematics to young children, defined the traditional approach as: 'Systemisation without a basis of ideas springing from experience.' They recognise that the new approach has dangers if it is not fully understood by the teacher, for they go on: 'Experience which children never build into an interrelated body of ideas would be equally unfortunate.'[24] There is no foolproof way of teaching mathematics.

Chapter 12
Discipline

What I have written in Chapter 1 and elsewhere about discipline is, I believe, both true and sensible; but, for several reasons, a chapter dealing specifically with the subject seems desirable. There is considerable anxiety not only among members of the general public but also among professional teachers about the indiscipline said to characterise an increasing number of English schools and taking the form of lack of respect for teachers, disobedience and sometimes violence. The complaints are chiefly concerned with the secondary schools (age twelve upwards) but they often attribute some of the blame to the 'permissive' primary schools from which the children come.

A recent example will serve as a model through which the whole situation can be examined. A young, inexperienced woman teacher had much difficulty with a boy in her class who was consistently impertinent, disobedient and unco-operative. At last, driven by exasperation, she bound his hands and put sticking plaster over his mouth. The boy's father sued the teacher in court for assault and battery. The magistrates found her guilty and fined her a substantial sum with costs.

This young teacher had to deal with the immediate problem of a disturbing influence in her class, of constant interruption and rudeness. I have much sympathy with what she did but I think she was wrong in using what were technically violent methods to control what was obviously deep-seated trouble. If violent methods are ever appropriate, which is doubtful, they should be confined to sporadic naughtiness and big-headedness. They never cure anything worse and they almost certainly make deep-seated trouble more difficult to cure. What the teacher ought to have done cannot be stated so definitely. It depends very largely upon the kind of school in which she was working and of this I have no knowledge. In a school in which the head teacher and staff have given to human relations the importance that they need and have really thought out what good relations imply, it is usually possible to 'contain' a difficult child by a variety of methods, which include team-work by the teachers, possibly psychiatric treatment, a constant dialogue between the teacher who is bearing the brunt and the head teacher, and a real consultation with the parents, so that the whole situation is brought to light and an attempt made to cure it and not simply to suppress it.

The correspondence in the Press which followed the case was mainly on the side of the teacher and contained criticism of the kind of educational approach commended in this book, though there was no evidence that the school was run on these lines at all. The burden of many letters was that progressive education was the brain-child of theorists who had somehow imposed their ideas on the unfortunate teachers who, in turn, in unthinking obedience, had imposed them on the children. These comments showed a very imperfect acquaintance with the English educational system and a tendency to oversimplify and to make suggestions which were claimed to be simple solutions of the problem. The problem has no simple solution.

The questions that really need answering in connection with the case are:

1 What had made this particular boy so difficult?

2 What was there in the father's own education and in his relations with his son's school which made him seek legal redress rather than talk the matter over with the teacher and headmaster?

3 Why were the magistrates so sympathetic to the father and so stern to the teacher?

4 What was there about the school which made the teacher seek this particular remedy rather than discuss the problem with her colleagues?

The problem must be looked at not simply in the context of the school but in that of the school and its relations with society. Where a school is seen by the children and parents who use it as a place in which the adults treat the children as people and show a readiness to listen and discuss as well as to teach and give orders, a place in which the rules are seen to be reasonable and necessary, a place in which the curriculum, or most of it, is clearly and unmistakably geared to the children's needs, there will be few disciplinary difficulties; and those that arise will be dealt with by the pressure of public opinion. Where, however, the school is looked upon as an alien place, though attended compulsorily, demanding automatic obedience to rules of which the reasonableness is often far from clear (short hair or no jewellery, for example), in which the curriculum is designed for the more able or with objectives that the majority do not seek, where the adults self-evidently belong to a different world whose values are not attractive or even relevant, there will be constant friction and this will certainly become worse in the future.

Another piece of evidence may throw light on the situation. The following is an extract from an article contributed by a sixteen-year-old girl to the *OZ* school kids' number:[25]

Were you born to be free? Free from the system, free from tradition. If you were, you are one of the minority and you are bloody lucky; but the rest of you what about you? This society is closing in on you and taking you over. It is a safe bet that you obey someone who is your equal but holds a higher position than you. Why not start a freedom campaign in your area now and do just as you wish? Whenever you feel like pissing in the street, then do it: if you feel like dancing at a funeral, then go ahead and do it. Live for the moment and not the future. Be free and tread on anyone who stands in your way. Your true identity is sure to come to the surface. Don't become Mr and Mrs Average. Live a little before it's too late.

Confronted with this piece of writing, adult readers have tended to take up one of three positions. The first is represented by some such comment as 'This vulgar, offensive writing is just what must be expected if children are given their heads, subjected to no discipline, taught no manners and encouraged "to express themselves".' The second is indicated by the view that this is simply the old game of shocking the grown-ups in which children have always indulged. It is not to be taken seriously. The only thing that is new about it is that someone has printed it. The third response is very different. It sees the writing, brash as it is, as a genuine symptom of a far-reaching change, a change which involves a revolt by the young against the values upheld by the older generation, and its publication as showing that some adults at least approve of this revolt and wish to aid and abet it.

All these three responses merit serious consideration in the context of discipline. Unless it is believed that the rows of well-behaved and respectful children who were, supposedly, character-istic of the old discipline never had rebellious or erotic thoughts, never used improper language or told 'dirty stories' when out of earshot and never secretly broke the rules, it must be admitted that relaxation of discipline will disclose and encourage behaviour which may be distressing to adults. A teacher who expects auto-matic respect and constant obedience from children is totally at a loss when he does not get it and generally falls back on anger and violence. If the ethos of the school is strong enough to make violence work, in the sense of effectively squashing the riotous and the evil-doer, then there may be the appearance of success: but at a heavy cost. The cost is also heavy if the whole situation deteriorates into disorder and anarchy. I shall try to sort out this dilemma later on.

The second response described above admits the substance of the first but does not find the writing shocking. It is in a limited way refreshing, simply because it lacks the portentous solemnity of the first and the third. Nevertheless, I cannot admire it. It is fundamentally cynical; it brushes the children aside and does not really make any attempt to understand them (there is a tolerance which is deadly). It is adopted by a considerable number of teachers who are often intelligent and able, who may be successful with the kind of children who are comparatively indifferent to teachers' personalities; but it is not of these teachers that children speak with respect or affection afterwards. 'They did not treat us as people' is the children's comment on such teachers.

The third response is the fashionable one and there is much sense in it. The young have always questioned the values of their elders—at any rate in western Europe—but not, perhaps, to the extent that they do now. Discipline in schools has to be seen in the context of social and economic change, of shifting political alignments, of the decay of organised religion and the vast growth of religiosity and perhaps of true religion that has accompanied it, of the world of Vietnam, of apartheid, of Mao Tse-tung, of black power, of the 'bomb'. It is not sensible in such a world to carry on in school just as if nothing much had happened since 1939. All good education has a subversive element in it and, if the young are asking awkward questions and making unpleasantly critical observations, this should be a matter for congratulation. If, on the other hand, they are not critical of themselves, if they too readily equate the state of being young with the condition of being in-fallible, not only the old but they themselves will be the sufferers. The tyranny of one's peers can be at least as ruthless as the tyranny of one's elders and betters. Freedom is not an unmitigated blessing.

Teachers have to deal with the problems of discipline as they arise. However ideal the school and its relationships may be, however understanding the staff, there will remain a residue of difficulties. A single child can disrupt and sometimes corrupt a group. Big-headedness can occur, and so can pig-headedness. It remains true that in dealing with children we are not dealing with saints or angels and, unhappily, in some schools we *are* dealing with thugs. The temptation to fall back on violence is at times very strong ('It is the only language they understand'); yet to use it is to establish it as an accepted means of communication and sometimes as the only one. To renounce it demands a great act of faith and sometimes almost superhuman patience but those who can find that patience and faith do not regret it.[26]

The question remains as to what authority the teacher ought to wield. I cannot accept that he should have none, and I believe that this view corresponds with the general consensus of opinion not only among adults but among children themselves. This natural and acceptable authority has been described by George Dennison.[27] He says:

Its attributes are obvious: adults are larger, more experienced, possess more words, have entered into prior agreements with themselves. When all this takes on a positive instead of a merely negative character the children see the adults as protectors and as sources of certitude, approval, novelty, skills. In the fact that adults have entered into prior agreements, children intuit a seriousness and a web of relations in the life that surrounds them. If it is a bit mysterious it is also impressive and somewhat attractive; they see it quite correctly as the way of the world and they are not indifferent to its benefits and demands ... (for a child) the adult is his ally, his model and his obstacle for there are natural conflicts too and they must be given their due.

This is a good description of what is right and necessary in primary schools. Obviously, as the children grow older and develop physically, it must be adapted to their particular needs and understanding. Teachers, like parents, have a hard lesson to learn.

I suppose that a reader might, at this point, expect or hope that some sort of formula for dealing with indiscipline might be forthcoming: Is a 'naughty' child to be sent to the head teacher, sent out of the room, detained after school, set an imposition, deprived of some privilege or pleasure, given a bad mark, reported to his parents, reasoned with, given a good talking to or what? These are questions which can only be answered in the context of the individual school and of the class or group of children with which any particular teacher is dealing and of the teacher himself. There is no formula, only a variety of expedients which must be used or rejected with judgement and insight. None of us, if we are honest, can say that we know how the boy in the story at the beginning of this chapter ought to have been dealt with. That could only be clear, if at all, in the particular context in which the story took place. None of us can say just how we would handle the writer of the *OZ* contribution. All we can hope is that our sympathy, courage and judgement would have been equal to the situation and that we should have been allowed to use them.[28]

Chapter 13
The teacher

It must be plain that the key figure in all that is recommended in this book is the teacher. All sorts of things have their importance, the design of buildings and equipment, the organisation of schools, the choice and supply of books and material, the composition of the curriculum, the method of teaching reading and many others; but the indispensable component, without which everything else is nearly useless, is a good teacher. Even if some of the teaching is handed over either to television or to some kind of programme, this remains true. The teacher in direct contact with the child is what really matters. All experience bears this out. No one who really knows schools and children would dispute it for a moment. Unfortunately many who pontificate on the subject of education seldom see the inside of a school for more than an hour or so and, from political or commercial motives or simply from sheer ignorance, uphold some other essential as the panacea which will put all to rights.

I do not mean that teachers are more important than parents. The upbringing and care given to children by their parents and the interest that the parents take in them and in their schooling are crucial, but parents are not inside the school context and teachers are. This book is about what happens in school and, although the children's response to this is closely connected with parental influence, it is controlled by the teacher and for this reason the teacher is properly described as the key figure.

To become and remain a good teacher, a man or woman must have the right initial training and the right in-service training. It is true that millions of people have some teaching ability and could, by practice alone, become good teachers. This has always been so and the more such people there are, the better. Some professional claims are a bit inflated. Nevertheless, training is, if not absolutely essential, highly desirable and no national system now could possibly function without it.

The changes in England began in the schools before they were adumbrated or recommended in most of the colleges of education. Under the influences of Froebel, of the McMillan sisters and of such individual thinkers as Susan Isaacs, Dorothy Gardner, Nancy Catty and A. S. Neill,[29] some of them operating in independent schools, teachers began to make changes on their own initiative. This situation was possible in England for reasons already given. It would be very difficult or nearly impossible in countries where the central control is strong and where teachers are not expected to strike out on their own and are not accustomed to doing so. In such conditions the initial move must be made centrally.

Training systems in different countries vary a great deal, much of the variation reflecting the history of the country and of its educational system. No system is for export as a package, and it would be not only arrogant but fruitless for me to try to set out an ideal course. Some indications of a course of professional training, designed to encourage the individual initiative which is the essential feature of the recommended change, may be usefully given, however.

The design of this book is an indication of what, in my opinion, this course must include. It must include a consideration of what is being rejected and why. To say or to imply to students that everything done up to now has been wrong would be impolitic even if it were true. The reasons for believing that change is necessary must be discussed and understood, and the changes recommended must be seen in relation to, and as developments from, what is being rejected. This will involve study of children, of their behaviour, of their ways of learning and of the psychological background from which the changes derive, so that the students can relate their experience and observations to a theoretical basis. How deep such theoretical study ought to go is a matter for discussion, but there is little disagreement that psychology should have a place in the professional course. To this most would add sociology, so that teachers may learn how to look at and understand the social, cultural and economic backgrounds of their children, and also philosophy, in the modern analytical sense, so that they may learn how to distinguish meaningful and non-meaningful statements. Some would also include linguistics, so that all teachers and not only language specialists understand something of how language works; and some educational history.

The importance and relevance of all these can hardly be disputed. The difficulty is how to fit them in with all the other requirements of a course without running the danger of superficiality. The mistake lies in the assumption made by many, including far too many teachers, that the initial course of training is somehow complete in itself instead of just an introduction to a vast field of knowledge which must be explored increasingly in all the years of their lives. 'Reading maketh a full man' and, if teachers are to be 'full men', they must regard reading and study as obligations.

The course must also include some knowledge of what happens in practice when the changes have been made. In a country such as England, where there is a substantial proportion of progressive schools, this is comparatively easy to arrange. I used to take students for whom I was responsible, who were doing a one-year course of professional training following a degree, to two progressive schools for one day each. These visits, which were quite separate from the teaching practice done by the students in schools of very varying kinds, followed on the theoretical and descriptive parts of the course so that the students knew something of what to expect. Naturally, some questions remained unanswered or partially answered, but the effect of these two short visits was quite dramatic. The students saw with their own eyes, and their confidence both in the soundness of the approach and in their own ability to use it was much increased.

In countries where there are no examples of progressive schools a different strategy must be followed, one much slower in achieving widespread results but essential as a first step. This is the setting up of experimental schools. It would be neither practical nor sensible to staff these with expatriate teachers imported for the purpose. It is much better to use from the very beginning indigenous teachers familiar with the language and customs of the country. But if this is done, two preliminary actions must be taken. First, a short course—a fortnight might be enough—should be mounted for the teachers concerned and staffed by expatriates either wholly or in part. Immediately afterwards the school or schools should be opened with the expatriates staying on as advisers or consultants. One such adviser for each school should perhaps remain for as long as a year and, when possible, should pay subsequent short visits from time to time until the schools are well established. At this stage it should be possible to evaluate the experiment and then to decide upon subsequent developments. Only if the teachers were con-convinced that the new approach, as it had evolved in the experimental schools, was suited to their capacities and ideals should the number of schools run on the new lines be increased. If they were not convinced, the experiment would have to be written off as a failure or be reconstructed and repeated in another part of the country. Any attempt to impose a system on reluctant and unconvinced teachers would be the rejection of all the principles that underlie it. At the same time those who are willing to experiment need every possible support from the central authority.

An important factor in the process of change is in-service training. Traditionally in England this has consisted simply of courses of varying length and kind, organised and staffed by HM Inspectors, by Local Education Authority organisers and, latterly, by Institutes of Education.[30] Attendance has always been voluntary and, though the quality of the courses has been high, they could not alone contribute more than a limited amount to the needs of the schools. Many teachers acknowledge that it was attendance at one of these courses which opened their eyes to the possibilities of change and started them upon a new path, but their total impact was necessarily restricted. Teachers do not receive extra pay for attendance, though for the longer courses they usually receive their expenses and are given leave of absence by their employers. In recent years the number of such courses has increased, but the most important development has been the setting up of the Schools Council,[31] the establishment of Teachers' Centres and the growing, if still slow, recognition by head teachers that one of their most important jobs is continuing the training of their staffs. Since all three of these developments seem to be possibilities in other countries, a brief account of each may be appropriate.

The Schools Council is a large body of more than eighty members, on which are represented all the interests in education, including the churches, industry and local government, but on which the teachers' organisations have an absolute majority. The Council works through sub-committees on all of which this teacher majority is maintained, thus making it impossible for the Council to embark on any project to which the teachers are opposed. The Council employs a salaried staff but none of them is permanent. It offers no career. All the principal officers are seconded for two or three years from one of the constituent bodies. The Council's budget is borne by the Department of Education and Science and until lately the joint secretaries have been seconded from that Department, one being an 'office' Civil Servant and the other one of HM Inspectors of Schools. A third joint secretary has recently come from the Inner London Education Authority.

The Council is concerned with curriculum and examinations. It is the former function which is relevant in the present context. The Council undertakes inquiries and surveys which are called Projects. When the appropriate sub-committee (Primary, Secondary, etc.) has chosen some particular topic and the Council has approved, a team is set up, variously composed but consisting generally of teachers, inspectors and academic specialists, some on full-time secondment, others part-time. This enables the team to keep in close touch not only with schools generally but with the particular schools in which part-time members work. English, French, mathematics, science and other fields have all been looked at in this way. The team thinks out new methods and ideas and tries them as it goes along so that, when its work is finished and a report has been prepared and teachers' material produced, the product will have been tested throughout the whole process by practising teachers in classrooms. The material is not a programme, though the danger of its becoming one is always latent. It is rather a set of suggestions and ideas which each individual must work out for himself and of course there is no compulsion, legal or moral, on any teacher or school to use it.

The Schools Council is thus a continuing means of studying all aspects of the curriculum, with teachers playing a major part and with the assistance of specialists drawn from Universities and Colleges of Education. The Council makes available to all teachers the outcomes of this study.

The number of teachers who can be involved in this work of the Council is necessarily limited. The Teachers' Centres, of which there are between five hundred and six hundred distributed all over the country and maintained by the Local Education Authorities, provide similar opportunities for a much larger number. These centres consist of one or two rooms, often in a disused school, with a small library, comfortably furnished, normally with a whole-time or part-time warden, where teachers can meet for all sorts of purposes, usually immediately after school hours, sometimes on Saturdays. They are not simply for lectures but rather for work and study.

One group of teachers, to which the writer belonged, was concerned with the development of spoken language in children. Questions were posed and each member undertook to try to find the answer with his own class. The group met fortnightly and at the second meeting some answers were reported and new questions raised. In due course some tentative conclusions were reached, all on the basis of the members' practical experience with children whom they knew and taught. At this stage the group invited a linguistics specialist from the university to jòin them and asked him whether the conclusions to which they had come accorded with his own knowledge of language. The result was most encouraging and the co-operation most fruitful. Finally a paper was drawn up and made available to any teachers who were interested.

The Centres are also used for increasing teachers' knowledge of a subject, notably mathematics, but here too there will be constant reference to teaching and learning as the members of the group experience them in their schools. The mathematics expert in charge of a primary group may himself be a secondary school teacher, unfamiliar with the problems of teaching young children but he will soon learn from his primary school colleagues, just as they will learn from him. The opportunity that the Centres provide for this co-operation between different phases of education which too often in the past have been separated is not the least of the benefits they have conferred.

Assistance to the teacher in the classroom itself, in England, has traditionally been provided by HM Inspectors and the inspectors and organisers employed by the Local Education Authorities. The relationship between the teachers and these official visitors has for many years been friendly and relaxed. It has been both a spur and an inspiration to the teachers and a means of spreading news of good practice and interesting experiment. It has always led to a certain amount, sometimes to a great deal, of discussion among school staffs and has been generally an instrument of innovation. Lately and increasingly head teachers have seen the in-service training of their staffs as an important part of their role, and they are now taking the initiative in this much more than was customary even a short time ago. Just how they do it varies. Some arrange visits to other schools, followed by discussion. Others have periodic staff meetings sometimes involving the discussion of a particular book or article which one teacher has read and been asked to comment on. Others work more informally, spending much of their time in the classroom working with the teachers. The aim in every case is to stimulate continuous thinking and dialogue about what is being done in the school.

To fulfil such a role successfully demands a great deal of tact and insight in a head teacher. He has to establish with his staff a relationship in which they respect his leadership and he their gifts and personalities. There is no formula for this relationship. It is certainly not authoritarian in any crude sense though it is not without the element of authority. Equally certainly it is not the flabby, negative 'I trust my teachers and let them do what they like' position adopted by some heads. The ideal is perhaps a team of friends led but not dominated by one. Where something like this has been achieved the best results have followed.

The essentials of the initial and in-service training could be mediated through a variety of systems and devices, and it must be for each country to determine just what these are to be. If, however, the objective is the kind of education upheld in this book, the following needs must be kept in mind and provided for in whatever system is established.

1 The teachers must have a firm grasp of the theoretical basis of the change.

2 They must have some experience of the changes in practice.

3 They must be educated to take the initiative together with the responsibility of doing so, and to submit what they do to their own critical analysis.

4 They must receive support in the form of in-service training, some of which must be internal, i.e. undertaken in individual schools by head teachers or, as a temporary measure, by visitors appointed for the purpose; and they must have the support of the central authority.

This chapter has been concerned with professional training in the restricted sense of pedagogy, methodology, practical skill and the like but it is implicit in all that has been said that this, by itself, will not make a teacher. In the free approach more than in any other the teacher must be an educated person. To define what this means so as to command general assent is not easy, perhaps impossible, and it is beyond the scope of this book to consider how such a person is 'produced'. Something must be said, however sketchily, about this requirement, even if the result is more like an educational sermon than a scientific analysis.

A teacher of young children must have a lively interest in people and the world about him and be well informed over as wide a field as possible. He must have resources which are continually fed from reading, conversation and, so far as possible, travel. The Elizabethan ideal of the all-round man is still the best model for the teacher to follow. If he is dull and indifferent and if his interests are restricted, he will be quite unable to share or to stimulate the enormous curiosity that children show when given the chance and will certainly show if given the kind of education here discussed.

But this is not enough. The teacher must have knowledge as well as information and the experience of disciplined study as well as a lively interest. Just how wide and how deep this knowledge and study are to go must depend upon individual capacity, upon the resources of the teacher's own education and upon the cultural and educational state of the society in which he belongs. Unless a teacher knows what it is like to study in depth, to explore a subject thoroughly, to discover what other minds have thought about it, he will have no standard by which to measure either his own capacities and limitations or his pupils', no scale against which his more superficial knowledge may be set. Furthermore, he may never learn the habit of reflection, of constantly turning over in his mind what his knowledge amounts to, of becoming an independent thinker, of using inductive and not only deductive thinking. Such thinking seems to spring most easily from a combination of knowledge in depth and wide interest and curiosity.

Even this is not enough. A teacher must be a moral person. I do not mean that he must conform to any particular moral code, but rather that he must see the kind of way in which he regulates his own conduct, the kind of person he is, as being an essential part of his role as a teacher. It is not possible to be a good teacher and a bad person. The influence of the person will always over-power the skill of the teacher. The values he holds as a person will in the end be those that he transmits to his pupils.

How these requirements—that of all-roundness, that of knowledge and study in depth, and that of morality—are to be met in the training system cannot be considered here. Each country must find its own road but, if the road misses any of them it will be, not perhaps the wrong road, but certainly not the best road to the destination.

Almost every social and technical development of our time has increased the importance of the teacher and especially of the primary teacher. The loosening of family ties, the diminishing hold of organised religion, the conurbation, the increased mobility and the spending power of the masses, mass production and automation, the coming of TV into every home, to name only a few, have all created for children, either directly or indirectly, an environment which is bewildering and insecure. For most children the school is the only place in which they may learn to come to terms with this environment, and the formative years before the age of twelve are precisely those in which this must be done. The low esteem in which the primary teacher is held in many countries is an indication of a failure by society to understand priorities. It is he who is the key figure in the educational process, and it is on the effectiveness of the educational process that the survival of society depends.

Notes

1 Brown and Precious: *The Integrated Day*, Ward Lock Educational, London, 1968, 1969, Agathon Press, New York, 1969.
See list of books for further reading, page 106.

2 See Plowden Report (*below*), Volume 2, Appendix 7.

3 *Handbook of Suggestions for the consideration of Teachers in Elementary Schools*, HMSO, London, 1905, 1909, 1918, 1926, 1937.

4 The Central Advisory Council is a statutory body which undertakes educational inquiries. Its personnel changes with each new inquiry and each particular inquiry, and the people who make it are referred to by the name of the Chairman concerned. The Plowden Council, under the chairmanship of Lady Plowden, sat from 1963 to 1966 and produced in 1967 *Children and their Primary Schools*, HMSO, commonly known as the Plowden Report.

5 Plowden Council: see above.

6 t.o. stands for Traditional Orthography, the alphabet in general use in Europe and America. i.t.a. (initial teaching alphabet) is a simple and extremely ingenious modification of t.o., designed by the late Isaac Pitman and developed by his grandson, Sir James Pitman, KBE. In it each letter has a constant sound. This makes the task of learning to read very much easier. It is in use in about thirteen to fifteen per cent of British infant schools and is spreading quite rapidly in other countries. For a full account and evaluation, see Warburton and Southgate: *i.t.a. An Independent Evaluation*, Murray and Chambers, London, 1969.
A recent development, of great importance to L2 learners of English, has been Speech i.t.a. In this, the use of light and heavy types makes it possible to show the accentuation of words and the *schwa* or neutral vowel which is so common in English.

7 R. S. Peters: *Education as Initiation*, Evans Bros., London, 1964.

8 B. F. Skinner: *The Technology of Teaching*, Appleton Century Crofts, New York, 1968.

9 *Mathematics in the Primary School* (Curriculum Bulletin No. 1), Schools Council, HMSO, London, 1964.

10 The Open University was set up in 1967 and began its teaching activities in 1971, having received a Royal Charter in 1969. It is for students of 21 or more, the majority in full-time employment. There are no required qualifications for admission. 'Maximum flexibility and an interdisciplinary approach . . . characterise Open University courses. Each course consists of correspondence packages, many of which call for

the return of assignments by students; a series of television and radio programmes; short summer or week-end courses; and regionally organised tutorial and counselling systems.' (The Open University *Prospectus 1972*. Open University, Bletchley, Buckinghamshire.)

11 Taylor: *Experiments with a Backward Class*, Methuen, London, 1948.

12 Local Education Authority (LEA). Education in Great Britain is mainly locally administered though subject to an overall national control.

13 I apologise for being unable to give the reference for this piece of research. I most culpably failed to make a note of it when I read it and strenuous efforts to track it down have failed.

14 The Plowden Report (above) recommended that selected areas of varying size where social and economic conditions were very unfavourable should be designated as Educational Priority Areas (EPAs) where intensive efforts would be made by means of staffing ratios, etc., to raise standards to the highest possible level. See Eric Midwinter: *Priority Education*, Penguin Books, London, 1972.

15 Catty: *Learning and Teaching in the Junior School*, Methuen, London, 1941.

16 *i.t.a. an independent evaluation*, F. W. Warburton and Vera Southgate, Murray and Chambers, London, 1969.

17 An interesting account of alphabetic history and of the genesis and use of i.t.a. may be found in *Alphabets and Reading*, Sir James Pitman and John St John, Pitman, London, 1969. i.t.a. is used by about 13% to 15% of primary schools. Very few teachers who have experience of it have willingly abandoned it. It is surprising, in view of the evidence, that its use has not become universal. To quote Professor Einstein: 'It is more difficult to disintegrate a prejudice than an atom.'

18 *op. cit.*

19 Private information.

20 The most useful book on the teaching of spelling is *Spelling taught or caught*, Margaret L. Peters, Routledge & Kegan Paul, London, 1967.

21 The quotation is from *Notes on Punctuation*, Eric Partridge, Blackwell, Oxford, 1955. See also the same author's *Usage and Abusage*, Hamish Hamilton, London, 1957.

22 *Breakthrough to Literacy*, David Mackay and Brian Thompson, Longmans, London, 1970 (for the Schools Council).

23 I made an attempt to provide some help and guidance to teachers in

this field in my *English Teaching for Non-specialists*, Faber, London, 1969. At the primary and middle stages it seems unlikely that most teaching of English will ever be in the hands of English specialists. It is the theme of this book that, with comparatively little trouble, the non-specialist general practitioner can make a positive contribution and need not, as too many do, fall back on a course book.

24 *Primary Mathematics Today*, Williams and Shuard, Longmans, London, 1970.

25 The 'underground' magazine *OZ* in May, 1970, published an issue known as 'The School Kids' Issue' which was entirely written and largely edited by children of secondary school age. The issue was the subject of a trial of the proprietors for obscenity in 1971. A full account may be found in Tony Palmer's *The Trials of Oz*, Blond and Briggs, London, 1971. The extract quoted is on page 47.

26 An absorbing account of two terms' work by a teacher who adopted this attitude in very difficult circumstances may be found in . . . *and softly teach* by Francis Lewis, A. & C. Black, London, 1971.

27 *The Lives of Children*, George Dennison, Random House, New York, 1969.

28 The chapter entitled 'Education for Docility' in Charles Sieberman's *Crisis in the Classroom*, Random House, New York, 1970, is full of interesting material on the subject of discipline.

29 Rachel (1859–1917) and Margaret McMillan (1860–1931) were pioneers in nursery education in England. On Rachel's death Margaret founded the Rachel McMillan Training College in her memory. The college is now a constituent of the London University Institute of Education.

Susan Isaacs founded an independent progressive school, The Malting House School, at Cambridge where many of the ideas in this book were first put into practice.

A. S. Neill (1885-1973) was founder and Headmaster of Summerhill School, Leiston, Suffolk, and author of many books.

30 Institutes (or Schools) of Education. There are seventeen of these institutions in England, each attached to a university, and every college of education is a member of one of them. They organise many different kinds of courses for serving teachers, some on a succession of winter evenings, some lasting for ten days or more during the summer vacation and some whole-time courses lasting for a year.

31 The Schools Council offices are at 160 Great Portland Street, London, W1N 6LL.

Further reading

There is a very large literature on primary schools. The following list is highly selective and may be seen as representing the next stage in reading after this book.

The most appropriate further reading is the series of pamphlets prepared under the joint auspices of the Schools Council (UK) and the Ford Foundation (USA), published in 1971 by Macmillan in the UK and by Academic Books in the USA. These are mainly descriptive, many of them being accounts by practising teachers of their own work. All are concerned with English primary schools.

Various authors: *Children at School*, Heinemann, London, 1969. An account of different aspects of English primary school life, written for CEDO with an African readership specially, though not exclusively, in mind. Each chapter has a short reading list.

John Blackie: *Inside the Primary School*, HMSO, London, 1967, 1968, 1969, 1972. This little book has sold 70,000 copies in the UK and the USA, and an American edition was published in 1971 by Schocken Books Inc., New York. It is intended for parents and the general public but has proved popular among teachers.

Arthur Razzell: *Juniors*, Penguin, London, 1968. A very readable book on rather similar lines, but confined to the 7–11 age-group.

Sybil Marshall: *Experiment in Education*, Cambridge University Press, 1963. A fascinating account of a tiny one-teacher school in a Cambridgeshire village.

J. A. and T. H. Simms: *From Three to Thirteen*, Longmans, London, 1969. The sub-title, 'Socialisation and Achievement in School', speaks for itself. An excellent account of the development of children.

Ruth Beard: *An Outline of Piaget's Developmental Psychology for Students and Teachers*, Routledge and Kegan Paul, London, 1969. Piaget's work is immense in bulk, and a shorter introduction to it is needed. There are several on the market of which this is perhaps the most generally useful.

Appendix I

The countries represented at the Weston-super-Mare seminar were: Argentina, Australia, Belgium, Canada, Chile, France, Ghana, India, Israel, Italy, Malaysia, Niger, Sweden, Switzerland, United Kingdom, USA, Zambia.

Appendix II

Reading standards in the United Kingdom

In 1948, in response to widespread assertions that reading standards had fallen, a body called the Interdepartmental Committee on Illiteracy carried out the first national reading test in the history of the United Kingdom. The test was devised for the occasion and was the joint work of Dr (now Professor) P. E. Vernon and HMI Dr A. F. Watts. It required the children, all 11 years of age, to read a number of sentences each having one omitted word and to choose from a list of five words the word which made the best sense in the blank space. The sentences went from easy to difficult, the easy ones requiring little more than the bare skill of reading, the difficult ones demanding the powers of interpretation involved in reading a *Times* leading article or something similar.

It was necessary, if the results were to be informative, to compare them with results from the pre-war period and this raised great difficulties. Pre-war tests and results had to be found which were reliable and the tricky process of calibration carried out, so that a score on the Watts-Vernon could be related to scores on the pre-war tests. No national pre-war test existed and finally only four tests were thought to be reliable, tests carried out in Glasgow by Dr Vernon, in Birmingham by Professor Schonell, in London by Sir Cyril Burt and in Leicester by Dr Cattell, all the testers, of course, being of the highest skill and reputation.

For a reason that has never been explained the Leicester results were not used, and the combined results of the three other cities, when compared with the 1948 results, showed that between 1939 and 1948 there had been a drop in the mean scores of 3·4. A point in this score represents 5 months so that this means a drop of about seventeen months in reading age. If Glasgow had been omitted and Leicester included (and no one has ever shown any reason why this would not have been equally valid), the result would have been a slight *improvement* during the war of 0·3, that is rather under two months.

These facts and figures illustrate how necessary is extreme caution in drawing conclusions. Common sense would suggest that the disturbance of bombing and evacuation did lead to some deterioration of standards, and my impression is that they probably did. But I was visiting infant schools in Manchester and Salford, two heavily bombed evacuation areas, in 1941–3 and the most striking feature was the great stability of the schools. That there was some deterioration I think is probable but that it was anything like seventeen months is most improbable.

Since 1948 the same test has been used four times and in each of the first three testings the mean score went up quite dramatically, thus:

1948	11·59
1952	12·42
1956	13·3
1964	15·00

that is an advance of seventeen months on 1948. In 1971 there was a drop of ·81 to 14·19, that is about four months.*

Those are the facts as far as we know them. The qualification is important. What is to be made of them? First of all, is the halt in progress attributable to the use of some particular method? When there is correspondence on the subject in the Press some correspondents invariably put the blame on 'Look-and-say', but there is not a scrap of evidence that method has anything to do with it, because the test was not administered so as to take any account of method. For the same reason the halt cannot be attributed to progressive methods generally. Progressive and traditional schools were not distinguished in the sample, for the very good reason that any definition of the two terms is too inexact to be usable in this kind of exercise.

At the time of writing a committee is sitting, under the Chairmanship of Sir Alan Bullock, who will report to the Secretary of State on the whole problem of reading standards and methods of teaching. The conclusions will be read with interest.

* See K. B. Start and B. K. Wells, *The Trend of Reading Standards*, London, NFER, 1972.

Index